ASHES,
CLASHES
AND BUSHY
TACHES

ASHES, CLASHES AND BUSHY TACHES

The talkSPORT Guide to Sport's Greatest Rivalry

Gershon Portnoi

SIMON &
SCHUSTER

London · New York · Sydney · Toronto · New Delhi

A CBS COMPANY

First published in Great Britain
by Simon & Schuster UK Ltd, 2013
A CBS Company

1 3 5 7 9 10 8 6 4 2

Simon & Schuster UK Ltd
1st Floor
222 Gray's Inn Road
London
WC1X 8HB

www.simonandschuster.co.uk

Simon & Schuster Australia
Sydney

Simon & Schuster India
New Delhi

A CIP catalogue for this book is available
from the British Library.

ISBN: 978-1-47112-850-9

Edited by Julian Flanders

Typeset and designed by Craig Stevens

Printed and bound in the UK by
Butler Tanner & Dennis Ltd, Frome, Somerset

Contents

● INTRODUCTION

If it wasn't for sport, what would we all actually do with our lives? When you've spent a moment considering that frightening thought, then imagine the hollow existence we would lead without being treated to a generous helping of Ashes cricket twice every four years (or twice in the same year, if 2013 is anything to go by).

It's not worth thinking about. That place is too dark. Instead, we should really spend a moment thanking Reginald Brooks and Lady Janet Clarke for creating the greatest, richest and most fascinating historical sporting rivalry in the world. For it was Brooks, a London-based journalist who penned the mock obituary for English cricket in the *Sporting Times* shortly after England had been defeated by Australia at The Oval in an amazing Test match – more about that later.

Brooks, perhaps also motivated by the political movement to permit cremation, which was illegal at the time, wrote the following mock obituary:

In Affectionate Remembrance
OF
ENGLISH CRICKET,
WHICH DIED AT THE OVAL
ON
29th AUGUST 1882,
Deeply lamented by a large circle of sorrowing
friends and acquaintances.
R. I. P.
N.B. – The body will be cremated and the
ashes taken to Australia.

This joke was seized upon by England captain Ivo Bligh, who pledged to bring back 'The Ashes' when he set sail for Australia a fortnight later. He repeated that promise on his arrival in Melbourne, even though nobody there would have had a clue what he meant, as there was no online version of the *Sporting Times* for them to read, nor any 24-hour sports news channel to keep a watching nation fully up-to-date with every latest quote. There wasn't even talkSPORT to spread the word. But the Aussie press soon latched on to the term (once it was explained) and that added extra interest to the series.

And then Lady Clarke and her governess Florence Morphy had a very bright idea. Bligh and his England team were staying at the Clarkes' Rupertswood estate in East Melbourne for Christmas before the three Test matches. A game was arranged on Christmas Eve between Bligh's men and members of her staff, which the English won. Lady Clarke then presented Bligh with a minuscule clay urn (rumoured to contain a burnt bail from this friendly game). She joked that he could now have those ashes back. There was an inscription on the gift which read:

> **When Ivo goes back with the urn, the urn;**
> **Studds, Steel, Read and Tylecote return, return;**
> **The welkin will ring loud,**
> **The great crowd will feel proud,**
> **Seeing Barlow and Bates with the urn, the urn;**
> **And the rest coming home with the urn**

Bligh kept the urn, England went on to win the Test series 2-1, and the captain also won himself a wife, Miss Morphy, whom he took back to England, along with the tiny urn, which remained at their home in Kent until his death in 1927, when it was donated to the MCC at Lord's where it can still be seen today.

Those metaphorical Ashes continued to be played for every time the countries met, but it was only in the 1998-99 series when a winning captain was actually presented with a replica urn to lift at the end of the contest – Australia's Mark Taylor being the first recipient.

Yet despite the absence of any real ashes, or even an urn, the ongoing rivalry between the two nations has remained constant and intense ever since those early days. The cricket writer Gideon Haigh once succinctly summed up England and Australia's relationship by writing here were 'two nations divided by a common game'.

Australia bowler Jason Gillespie, who was part of three Ashes-winning teams (and one losing side, but let's not dwell on that) was brutally honest about the meaning of the Ashes when interviewed for this book: 'Everyone can talk up rivalries about all the other countries that play each other, but everyone knows that Test cricket is about the Ashes. It's as simple as that.' His comments are echoed by former teammate Merv Hughes, when quizzed for this book, who said: 'There's only two nations in the world that promote Test cricket, and that's England and Australia.'

They're both right. If you're English or Australian, Ashes series have the ability to temporarily stop the world from spinning. When Aussie prime minister Sir Robert Menzies received a cable from British foreign secretary Anthony Eden about a conference scheduled for London in January 1953, he replied: 'No. What about June? Isn't there anybody on your staff who reads cricket fixtures?'

It didn't take long before Eden cabled back with: 'Point taken. Conference confirmed for day after Lord's Test.'

And the BBC reported that prime minister Tony Blair followed the gripping 2005 Ashes series 'ball by ball', although when you consider that went on all summer, you have to wonder who was actually running the country at the time.

But perhaps what sums up the rivalry best of all is a cultural point that Menzies noted: 'Great Britain and Australia are of the same blood and allegiance and history and instinctive mental processes. We know each other so well that, thank Heaven, we don't have to be too tactful with each other.'

And that's a message that many Ashes teams seem to have taken on board – that wonderful lack of tact which has given rise to so many amusing exchanges between rival players on the pitch, and equally jocular moments off it. It doesn't take much for Merv Hughes to snarl, Ricky Ponting to throw the toys out of the pram and Harold Larwood to try to kill an Australian every time he bowls. Which is precisely why this book, a comprehensive guide to the most humorous, bizarre and dramatic moments in Ashes history, had to be written.

So sit back, relax and enjoy a perfect blend of swearing, fighting, sledging, drinking and very hairy upper lips that only the Ashes can produce. There may even be a little bit of cricket in here somewhere, too.

● GLOSSARY

Ashes – nobody really knows, but our best guess is that these are the remains of a burnt bail in a friendly match that took place before the 1882-83 Australia v England Test series. And now every series, the teams play to win a tiny urn containing those burnt bail remains, even though they never actually get their hands on that urn, because it has been kept at Lord's since 1927.

Aussie – an abbreviation for an Australian, normally referring to a happy-go-lucky type of character who can instantly become an aggressive lunatic when a bat or ball is placed in his hand.

Bodyline – the polite term used for the attempted murder of Australian batsmen by English bowlers in the 1932-33 series.

Pom/Pommies – the Australian vernacular for an Englishman/group of Englishmen, most commonly used to describe those dressed in white who attempt to play cricket while maintaining stiff upper lips at all times.

Series – a load of games (usually at least five) in which grown men act as petulantly as children in order to try to win a tiny urn which they don't actually ever receive because it's always kept at Lord's.

Sledge – either a vehicle on runners for conveying passengers over snow or, in this case, an insult or jibe used to try to distract or humiliate an opposition player.

Tache – an abbreviation for moustache, which is the growth of upper-lip hair usually, but not always, on a male human.

Test – a thorough five-day examination of who is the very best at either throwing a red leather ball towards three sticks, or hitting that red leather ball away from those three sticks.

Tour – a two-month holiday taken by a group of Englishmen or Australians during which they occasionally have to be interrupted by playing a Test.

Urn – a vessel usually used for storing the ashes of a cremated person.

2005 – the year in which most England cricket fans believe the Ashes series of matches started.

CHAPTER ONE

ASHES FEVER

Twice every four years, doctors in both England and Australia become inundated with patients complaining of acting irrationally, becoming over-excited and generally feeling rather juvenile. This epidemic has become known as 'Ashes Fever' and is the result of over-exposure to Ashes Test matches and the hype surrounding them. It can affect players, spectators, umpires and even team officials. This chapter celebrates some classic cases of Ashes Fever, where those who should really have known better just couldn't help but be carried away by the drama of the Ashes.

● PRE-ASHES FEVER

One of the first recorded cases of Ashes Fever actually came about before the Ashes had been invented – or, to be more accurate, it was the event that created the Ashes.

W.G.Grace was the guilty man, as he ran out Australia's Sammy Jones after the batsman had left his crease to pat down a divot on the pitch during the 1882 Oval Test. This unsporting conduct enraged the Australia team, in particular demon fast bowler Frederick Spofforth, who confronted Grace in the changing rooms and called him 'a bloody cheat', among many other Australian pleasantries. As he left, he informed Grace: 'This will lose you the match.'

This seemed a bold and unlikely claim at the time, as England required only 85 to win, but a fired-up Spofforth took seven for 44 as the hosts were bowled out for 77. This shocking defeat led to the famous *Sporting Times* mock obituary announcing the death of English cricket and the Ashes was born. The rest, as they say, is history.

● SID'S STUMPED

What's that they say about 'it ain't over 'til it's over'? Australia's Sid Barnes was leading his side's charge to an easy victory in the first Test at Trent Bridge in 1948. He glanced a ball to the leg-side boundary for the winning runs before grabbing a stump and running joyfully off the pitch, followed by his batting partner Lindsay Hassett, the England fielders and the umpires.

As the players made their way off the pitch, the crowd began howling at them and it soon became apparent that the tourists were actually one run short of their target and Barnes had rather spectacularly jumped the gun, no doubt caught up in the excitement of winning (or not) an Ashes Test.

Moments later, the players returned to the field, followed by a rather grumpy and red-faced Barnes with his stump and his bat. He offered the bat to the umpire to place into the ground and made as if to take guard with the stump – a nice try, but not quite enough to hide his embarrassment.

And, to really rub salt into the wound, Hassett eventually struck the real winning shot and Barnes, running through to complete the run, failed to claim a souvenir stump.

● DON'T GAMBLE ON GLENN

Of the many differences between English and Australian cricketers, an over-abundance of confidence – otherwise known as sheer ballsiness – ranks highly on one side.

Australia's fast bowler Glenn McGrath is the perfect example to demonstrate this not so subtle distinction, with his world-famous Ashes predictions, which began in 2005 when he confidently declared the Aussies would win the series 5-0, barring rain intervening to prevent the inevitable from happening.

Strangely, what Mystic McGrath didn't predict was that it would be a largely dry English summer, or that he would tread on a cricket ball in the warm-up before the second Test at Edgbaston and damage ankle ligaments which would cause him to miss two matches, and that England would take advantage of his absence to go on to win one of cricket's greatest-ever series 2-1.

Thankfully, after that embarrassment, McGrath learned his lesson and was never so foolish as to... Hang on, this is the very same demon paceman at the start of England's 2006-07 tour:

'I reckon it will be five-nil this time, as well,' he told the *Mail on Sunday*. 'To say anything else would be negative. If we're going to win two-one, or three-two, which games are we going to lose?' And to reinforce the point and massage his own ego at the same time, McGrath added: 'England are not as strong as they were last year, but Australia are a lot stronger. And I'm fit, unlike last time. Put it this way, in the three Tests I played in last time, we drew two and won one.'

Those England fans hoping that such statements would bring him bad karma were to be disappointed. Amazingly, McGrath struck it second time lucky as England succumbed to only the second-ever Ashes whitewash (1920-21 being the other occasion, fact fans).

Come the 2009 series, McGrath had finally stopped tormenting England batsmen and hung up his boots, but that wasn't going to stop him calling the series – and guess what he went for? 'My prediction is it will be five-nil to Australia. I've got total confidence in the boys.'

Unfortunately for McGrath, that confidence was entirely misplaced as England once again ran out 2-1 winners, but he was at it again the following year when England returned to Australia to defend the Ashes: 'I'm still going with the five-nil. I can't really say anything else now, I guess I've dug a bit of a hole for myself, but I've got total faith in our boys.' England duly won the series 3-1, but McGrath was certainly right about one thing – he had dug a bit of a hole for himself.

Good call, Glenn.

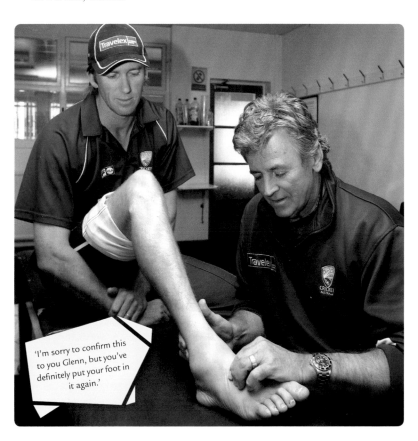

'I'm sorry to confirm this to you Glenn, but you've definitely put your foot in it again.'

● TERRY TAKES A TUMBLE

Australians don't like losing. And they definitely don't like being thumped on the head by an English spectator while fielding for a fifth straight session as the Pommie Ashes holders grind their way past 400 (Chris Tavaré was stuck on 66 for 90 minutes in one paint-drying period). We know this is true because Terry Alderman's reaction to this very scenario tells us so.

In 1982-83's first Test at Perth, English spectators invaded the pitch in celebration at their side passing the landmark, while Australia had roasted in the field for the best part of two days in temperatures of more than 100 degrees. Unfortunately, these England fans had been drinking in that heat and one of them, 19-year-old Gary Donnison, appeared to be slightly inebriated as he charged past Alderman (whose mood can't have been lightened by just being edged for four by England tailender Bob Willis) and clumped him on the head.

Said Alderman at the time: 'I have played a bit of Aussie Rules and I know what a gentle tap is and what a thump to the head is, and that was a thump to the back of the head.'

And it clearly affected his thinking as the bowler gave chase to Donnison, launched himself at him and the pair began wrestling on the WACA turf before Allan Border and Dennis Lillee dragged the Englishman away and pinned him down. [Note to younger readers: this actually happened!]

The problem for Alderman was that in performing his swan dive on top of his assailant, he managed to dislocate his shoulder, which not only ruled him out of the entire series but also kept him out of the game for a year. However, while he may have lost the battle, Lillee, Border and their fellow soldiers won the war, as the Aussies ran out 2-1 series winners.

Donnison, meanwhile, was fined $500 and ordered to do 200 hours of community service. He eventually became a born-again Christian. Seriously.

● LOOK AT WHAT YOU COULD'VE WON

So you're playing for Australia in the 1981 Ashes. Your team have racked up 401 for nine declared, bowled the Poms out for 174 and then reduced them to 135 for seven in their second innings, still 92 runs behind.

Do you a) Rub your hands at the prospect of taking a 2-0 lead in the series and break out into a chorus of 'Waltzing Matilda', or b) Place a bet on the opposition winning at the staggering odds of 500-1? Naturally, Dennis Lillee and Rodney Marsh plumped for option b).

Their team bus driver Peter Tribe placed the bets for them (£15 in total, a tenner from Lillee, a fiver from Marsh) with Ladbroke's at Headingley and, after heroics from Ian Botham with the bat and then Bob Willis with the ball, England became only the second team in history to win a Test after following on, while Lillee and Marsh suddenly became £7,500 richer. However, they were subsequently fined by the Australian Cricket Board for their lucky punt, leaving Tribe as the biggest winner (apart from England, of course) after the pair bought him a new set of golf clubs and a holiday to Australia.

Looking back on the incident, Lillee has remained typically forthright about his conduct. Writing in the *West Australian* newspaper, he said: 'Being a small-time punter, I had been unable to resist the juicy 500-1. It was as simple as that. I have never had any qualms over the matter and I have never lost a moment's sleep because of it.'

● CHASING THE CAT

The 1994-95 Ashes series had barely broken sweat when Phil Tufnell caught the bug – to be more accurate, it probably wasn't just the Ashes which caused England captain Mike Atherton to admit that Tufnell's 'room had been trashed and my left-arm spinner was in a sorry state'.

England were playing a tour opener in Perth and Tuffers was experiencing some difficulties in his personal life, having recently been beaten with a brick by his partner's father. It didn't take long before Ashes Fever also set in: Tufnell destroyed his room and was carted off to a local psychiatric unit.

But all was not as it seemed, as the man himself told the *Independent* in his inimitable style: 'It was quite funny, really. They took me off to this bleeding nuthouse and this bloke comes in and says, "Tell me about your childhood" and I think, "What am I doing here?" So I just legged it out with all these blokes running after me. I got myself back to the hotel, got myself a beer, went into the team room and said, "Sorry about that, chaps. See you at breakfast tomorrow morning."'

As is the prescription with so many of these cases of Ashes Fever, Tufnell was duly fined.

The one and only Phil Tufnell with chasing psychiatrists out of shot.

● GOADING GRAHAM

The normally unflappable Mike Atherton once let his guard down after Graham Thorpe fluffed a great chance to remove Matthew Elliott at Headingley in 1997.

Australia, 2-1 up in the series, had been wobbling at 50 for four when Elliott and Ricky Ponting came together. Mike Smith, playing in his only Test, induced an edge that carried to the normally reliable Thorpe, who spilled it. Elliott was on 29 at the time and went on to make 199 and add 268 with Ponting.

As England headed to defeat, Atherton told the guilty first slip: 'Don't worry Thorpey, you've only cost us the Ashes!'

'Athers used to wind me up about it,' admits Thorpe. 'That was probably the worst catch I've dropped in my career – or one of the most important catches. I'm not saying we would have won the Ashes, but it didn't help in that Test match. I got a bit of stick in the newspapers for it, but we always had banter in the dressing room. You have to have a sense of humour and a thick skin.'

● THE PHANTOM RAINFALL

Back in 1896, the touring Australians would have required extremely thick skin to take their hosts' Ashes Fever-induced behaviour on the chin.

In the deciding Test at The Oval, England were in trouble at the close on 60 for five, with a lead of just 86. No rain was forecast overnight and none came, leaving the Australians shocked at the conditions when they arrived at the ground the following morning. As opening batsman Joe Darling noted in his autobiography, 'One can well imagine our surprise when we found that there had been a "local rain" of about 22 yards long and 6 feet wide, just where the wicket was.'

With the pitch having been watered, England collapsed to 84 all out, but the Aussies never even came close to their target of 111 as England's bowlers made the most of the 'advantageous' conditions to rout the tourists for 44. Though, in fairness, it should be pointed out that 24 wickets had fallen on the second day after plenty of rain on day one.

● FALLING ON DEAF EARS

Those who question the morals of modern-day cricketers for not walking, claiming dodgy catches and appealing for anything and everything, might like to know t'was ever thus. The older generation had no moral high ground whatsoever, as is shown by the extraordinary behaviour of England wicketkeeper Bill Storer in the 1897-98 Sydney Ashes Test.

It was the opening game of the series and the Aussies were following on, with deaf batsman Charlie McLeod having made a steady 26 in a total of 135 for one, when he was bowled by a no ball. McLeod didn't hear the umpire's call and, as he made off towards the pavilion, Storer pounced to remove the bails and run him out.

England went on to win the Test, but that was to be their only victory of the tour as McLeod took brutal revenge with a century in the next Test, a five-wicket haul in the third and two more half-centuries in the last two matches to help the Aussies claim the series 4-1.

● ANYTHING GOES FOR GOWER

The 1989 Ashes series is fondly remembered by Australians, while the English like to pretend it never took place. With England coming into the contest holding the urn, few would have predicted the eventual 4-0 thrashing dished out by the Aussies (with the possible exception of Glenn McGrath).

England captain David Gower came in for plenty of stick from the press for his role in the debacle – from the minute he inserted Australia in the first Test at Headingley and they responded by posting 601 for seven declared, the writing was on the wall.

And by the third day of the second Test at Lord's, Gower had clearly had enough of the criticism. England were staring down the barrel of another defeat as they trailed by 184 with seven second-innings wickets remaining, and a stormy post-match press conference saw Gower succumb to an unusual strain of Ashes Fever.

It was particularly unusual for such a laid-back character – in England's Ashes victory in 1986-87, Gower was underneath a potential match-winning catch to dismiss Dean Jones. Captain Mike Gatting bellowed 'Catch it David!' across the pitch, which he duly did before jogging in with the ball and calmly telling his skipper: 'There's no need to shout.'

Back at Lord's and facing a barrage of questions about his tactics, Gower became irritated so simply stood up and told the assembled reporters that he had a taxi to catch for a West End show. The England captain had been invited to a preview of Cole Porter's *Anything Goes* and was determined not to miss it.

It must have been a decent show as he returned after the rest day (yes, they used to have them in those days) to make a battling century, but it wasn't enough to save England from defeat.

By the fifth Test at Trent Bridge, Gower and England's goose was well and truly cooked, but that didn't stop him from amusing himself when, after failing to take a wicket the entire first day and with Australia's first innings reaching 500 for two, he sent England's twelfth man Greg Thomas to the press box to ask the assembled journalists who they thought should bowl next.

● GO, SELECTOR

It wasn't just Gower who succumbed to Ashes Fever that summer – England's chairman of selectors also caught the bug.

Australia were able to use just 12 players over the course of the series, while Ted Dexter presided over a selection policy which ensured that a staggering 29 players featured during the six-match contest. Not just that, Dexter also managed to call England's new paceman Devon Malcolm, Malcolm Devon, and went on to claim he was entirely blameless for the debacle: 'I am not aware of any errors I have made this summer.'

Four years later, Dexter was at it again, when England lost at Lord's to fall 2-0 behind in the series, he said: 'The whole of our national sport is not doing very well. We may be under the wrong star sign. Venus may be in juxtaposition with somewhere else.'

Unsurprisingly, he was somewhere else by the end of the year.

● UP, UP AND AWAY

In between those two English domestic Ashes catastrophes (or catASHtrophes if you like), Gower went Down Under, with Graham Gooch captaining the tourists. But it was clear that the power of the returning Ashes Fever was too much for the former skipper to handle, judging by his actions during a tour match against Queensland.

With the Ashes already safely lost, Gower persuaded teammate John Morris to join him in flying two Tiger Moth airplanes during the game. Shortly after Robin Smith had completed his century, the pair flew over the Carrara Oval and were saluted by Smith and his batting partner Allan Lamb.

Their teammate Jonathan Agnew recalled that 'everyone found it funny except Graham Gooch' but, unfortunately for Gower and Morris, the England management fined them £1,000 for the escapade. As *Guardian* cricket correspondent Mike Selvey pointed out at the time, there was a far worse breach of discipline earlier in the tour, when two players had returned from a night out at 1am during the first Test – the problem for Gower was that he was one of those players.

England's new batting helmets failed the health and safety examination.

● AN APPLE A DAY

Monty Noble was an Australian cricketer who bored English fans to tears with his stubborn refusal to give away his wicket.

Once, in the Old Trafford Test of 1899, he made an unbeaten 60 and 89 while batting for almost nine hours – during his time at the crease, impatient spectators began singing 'The Dead March' while one fan became so exasperated he bellowed: 'Put a rope around the bounder's neck and drag him out!'

None of that fazed Noble, who had performed his most amazing feat on board the ship from Australia to England as it was passing through the Suez Canal. Someone on the docks was seen making obscene gestures at the female passengers on board, so Noble took an apple and hurled it fully 80 yards to strike a blow on the offender which ensured there would be no more lewdness from that particular Suez worker.

● ANGRY ALLAN

At first glance, Allan Border's reaction to a cheap dismissal against England in the Perth Test of 1979 seems entirely normal. Having been trapped LBW by Ian Botham for just 4, you can understand how angry Border would have been.

You can understand how he climbed the steps to the dressing room with the failure weighing heavily on his mind. You can understand how he barged into the dressing room door with his shoulder to make a deliberately angry entrance.

You can understand how he hurled his bat to the floor then threw off his batting gloves and kicked them as far away as possible. You can understand how he launched into an expletive-laden verbal assault on England, the English and their cricketers.

What you, like Border, probably can't understand, however, was why he was actually in the England dressing room.

● ANGRIER ALLAN

When Border arrived in England for the 1993 series, he set his stall out to be as businesslike as possible from the off.

Pretty much as soon as he had set foot in the country, he was gripped by Ashes Fever and told assembled journalists: 'I am not talking to anyone in the British media. They are all pricks.'

● ONE BRINGS TWO

It's always vital for teammates to believe in each other if they are to be successful – or so we are told.

Australia's stand-in captain Vic Richardson was leading the 1930 tourists in a match against Glamorgan in Swansea. Whenever an Australia wicket fell, the public address system announcer would ask Richardson the identity of the new batsman and duly share that information with the spectators.

However, when the eighth wicket fell, Richardson informed the PA man that Wall was coming in next, but that he might as well announce Wall and last man Walker together, because the pair of them wouldn't last long.

Seconds later, with Wall on his way to the crease and Walker padding up, the PA system repeated Richardson's quip to the general amusement of all at the Swansea ground. And to illustrate his point perfectly, three balls later the innings was indeed over – the team spirit clearly wasn't affected though, as the tourists went on to win the Ashes series 2-1.

● ACTION FACTION

The fifties was an Ashes decade full of controversy over suspect bowling actions and its associated Ashes Fever reached its peak during England's 1958-59 tour – and even the officials weren't immune on this occasion.

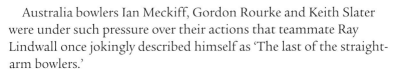

Australia bowlers Ian Meckiff, Gordon Rourke and Keith Slater were under such pressure over their actions that teammate Ray Lindwall once jokingly described himself as 'The last of the straight-arm bowlers.'

In one match, Fred Trueman and some of his England colleagues were involved in a conversation with an umpire as Slater's action was called into question. The official smiled and said: 'Well, at least he's chucking straight, isn't he mate?'

● GETTING THE 'UMP-IRE

In the days of home umpires, some of them loved to rise to the challenge of officiating in the Ashes – assuming that challenge was to match the intensity of their compatriots on the pitch.

In the 1990-91 Melbourne Test, England were (unsurprisingly) on their way to another defeat and spinner Phil Tufnell was toiling away on his maiden Ashes tour, desperate for his first wicket. He innocently asked umpire Peter McConnell how many balls remained in the over.

'Count 'em yourself, you Pommie bastard!' replied the umpire. Mayhem ensued as captain Graham Gooch became involved telling the official he couldn't talk to his players like that. Shortly after, David Boon appeared to edge a Tufnell delivery into wicketkeeper Jack Russell's gloves and, as Tufnell celebrated, McConnell interrupted him with a firm 'Not out'.

'You f**king bastard!' screamed Tufnell.

'Now, *you* can't talk to *me* like that!' replied the umpire.

● GETTING THE BIRD

English umpire Dickie Bird usually kept his composure, even in the heat of battle. The eccentric Bird often had to deal with abuse from spectators, who used to blame him for the weather even when the official had no choice but to bring the players off the pitch.

On one occasion during an Old Trafford Ashes Test match, Bird, followed by the Australia batsmen and England fielders, left the field. As he arrived in the pavilion, one particularly drunk spectator, clearly also consumed by Ashes Fever, berated Bird, saying: 'You're 'ere again. Every time you come to Old Trafford you're always bringing 'em off. Surely it's not bad light? The sun's shining!'

Bird looked at the man, who was finding it hard to even stand, before replying: 'No, sir. It's lunchtime.'

● SIDDLE SIZZLES IN THE MIDDLE

There is no doubt that the media saturation of Ashes coverage in recent years has only served to cause even more widespread outbreaks of Ashes Fever. Such was the hype surrounding the 2010-11 series in Australia, both sets of players were at each other's throats with the verbals from the word go – or 'play' to be accurate.

By the time of the Perth Test, the tension had almost got out of hand, as Peter Siddle and Matt Prior locked horns in the middle. The England wicketkeeper was subjected to a barrage of brutal bowling and mouthy maulings from Siddle, who finally dismissed Prior with a ball which hit his body and then the stumps.

The Aussie continued to bait Prior as he left the wicket, causing the Englishman to lose the plot and, according to some accounts, he was heard to say: 'Come with me, let's have it right now. Let's go outside right now!' while gesticulating in the direction of the pavilion.

Prior later denied having offered his opponent out. He wrote in his column in the *Independent*: 'As I left he said something that annoyed me. There are not many boxing matches when a guy knocks someone out and then kicks him while he's on the floor.

That isn't the way it works. Having said that, I didn't need to react in the way I did. What has been reported that I said is not true. I didn't offer to take him into the car park or offer to fight him after the game. I didn't say anything along those lines.'

● ALL HILL BREAKS LOOSE

We mere mortal cricket fans are not usually privy to the goings-on in the sacred inner sanctum of a selectors' meeting – and perhaps that's just as well given the events in the offices of the New South Wales Cricket Association in Sydney in 1912.

The gathering was to pick the team for the fourth Test in a series that had not been going well for Australia, who had lost the two previous matches. One of the selectors, former player Peter McAlister, had a long-running feud with Aussie captain Clem Hill and made several jibes at him during the meeting, criticising his captaincy. Hill replied that McAlister was 'no judge of cricket' and the selector countered that he was as 'good a captain as Armstrong, Trumper or you'.

The quickfire exchange was rapidly spinning out of control, as Hill told McAlister he knew nothing about cricket, only for the selector to hit back by telling Hill he was 'the worst captain in living memory'.

Hill stood up and informed McAlister, 'You've been asking for a punch all night and I'll give you one.' Incredibly, the captain then hit the selector before a no-holds barred brawl broke out, during which Hill had to be stopped from throwing McAlister out of the third-floor window.

After leaving McAlister bloodied and bruised, Hill left the meeting and, even more incredibly, was picked as captain for the Melbourne Test. Unfortunately for him and Australia, two more defeats were dished out by England.

Perhaps McAlister was right ...

● THE CHANT WARS

There's probably no finer example of Ashes Fever than the emergence of England's 'Barmy Army' supporters and 'The Fanatics', their Australian counterparts.

The Barmy Army first arrived on the scene during the 1994-95 Ashes and are fondly regarded by the players. 'The first Ashes tour I went on was in 1994-95 and that was the first time that the Barmy

Army came along,' recalls Graham Thorpe. 'They'd just started off and followed us all round Australia, making all their songs up. Although we lost the series three-one, they were still good memories.'

Which brings us to those songs. When they're not repetitively chanting 'Barmy Army', they have a huge back catalogue of ditties about players past and present, and have now branched out into songs that will deliberately wind up opponents. This is the Barmy Army's version of Aussie anthem 'Waltzing Matilda':

What David Gower's brother lacked in cricket talent, he made up for in hair.

We all shagged Matilda
We all shagged Matilda
We all shagged Matilda
And so did our mate

And she moaned and she groaned
As she took it up the billabong
We all shagged Matilda
And so did our mate

And they had arguably less respect for Mitchell Johnson, the Australia bowler who struggled with his line throughout both the 2009 and 2010-11 series, singing this to the tune of 'Sloop John B':

> He bowls to the left,
> He bowls to the right,
> That Mitchell Johnson,
> His bowling is sh*te

The Australian fans have created some similarly insulting songs including their own version of 'Bohemian Rhapsody' for the 2005 series that included the line:

> Brett Lee just killed a man,
> Bowled a ball around his head,
> Hit his temple,
> Now he's dead

And the players don't seem to mind too much either, with Lee explaining the song: 'The batsman was of course Freddie [Flintoff], but I'm sure he didn't mind as it was all in good fun.'

Anything goes with Ashes Fever.

● LANGER'S DOSSIER DISASTER

Ahead of the 2009 Ashes series in England, former Aussie opener Justin Langer decided to issue the tourists with a dossier to increase their chances of success. Naturally, this document was leaked to the press, and it wasn't long before the England team were reading Langer's musings, which no doubt gave them that extra bit of motivation throughout the summer.

Langer, a fiery character on the pitch, was no less forthright in his musings as his dossier included: 'English players rarely believe in themselves. Many of them stare a lot and chat a lot but this is very shallow. They will retreat very quickly. Aggressive batting, running and body language will soon have them staring at their bootlaces rather than in the eyes of their opponent – it is just how they are built.'

Needless to say, England won the series.

● A FLAT DAY'S PLAY

In these days of spectators arriving at Test matches in full fancy dress costumes, it's hard to find a genuinely unusual sight in the grandstands. But in Adelaide in 1986-87, one spectator provided a truly bizarre vision that would even raise eyebrows today.

It was the fifth day of a match that was heading for a draw and one woman, suffering from an extreme bout of Ashes Fever, spent all three sessions of the match doing the ironing. As *Wisden* noted: 'A female spectator set up an ironing board and attended to her laundry throughout the fifth day's play.'

She clearly had no other pressing matters to attend to.

Sorry.

● ACTING WITHOUT GRACE

Not many players can claim to have represented England and Australia in Test matches. In fact, there are just five who have done so. But only one of them can also lay claim to having been kidnapped from Lord's during a match, in an early case of Ashes Fever.

Billy Midwinter was born in St Briavels, Gloucestershire, before emigrating to Australia with his parents, where he eventually played against a touring English team led by W.G.Grace in 1873. The doctor was so impressed that he tried to persuade Midwinter to play for his county of birth, but in the first Test of 1877, he lined up for Australia, becoming the first man to take five wickets in an innings. He went on to represent England in four Tests on their

1881-82 tour of Australia, before lining up for Australia again in the first match of the 1882-83 series.

Before all that, Midwinter came back to England to play county cricket alongside Grace in 1877, but trouble brewed the following season when the Australians included him in their 1878 touring team.

Arriving at The Oval for a Gloucestershire fixture against Surrey, Grace was appalled to hear that Midwinter was across the city at Lord's with the tourists for a game against Middlesex. He promptly summonsed a taxicab to St John's Wood where he strode into the pavilion and frog-marched a padded-up Midwinter straight out of Lord's and into the waiting cab. Incredibly, the Australians gave chase all the way back to The Oval, where they became embroiled in what we're reliably informed back then was 'fisticuffs' with Grace.

Not only did the Englishman manage to fight them off, he also made sure Midwinter stayed with Gloucestershire for the rest of the summer.

● ENGLAND'S TWELFTH MEN

Occasionally, a bout of irrational Ashes Fever can be used to positive effect, as was the case in the final Ashes Test of 1968 at The Oval. The tourists had already retained the Ashes, but England had a chance to earn a series draw, with the Aussies in trouble at 86 for five at lunch on the final day, requiring an unlikely 352 for victory.

A huge thunderstorm then rendered the pitch unplayable and seemed to have ended England's hopes; but hundreds of eager home fans stiffened their upper lips, rolled up their trouser legs and began mopping up the outfield with blankets, towels and handkerchiefs and, remarkably, play restarted later that afternoon.

In the short time remaining, slow left-armer 'Deadly' Derek Underwood, took four of the five remaining wickets to lead England to victory with just five minutes to spare.

● McGRATH IN THE MIDDLE

Even when you reach the end of the road and are playing in your final Test, Ashes Fever can still take hold. Australia were coasting to victory in the final Test of the 2006-07 series, which was also Glenn McGrath's swansong. Chasing just 46 to win, openers Justin Langer and Matthew Hayden were easing the Aussies home when captain Ricky Ponting turned to McGrath, nicknamed Pigeon, and said: 'You're batting at three today, Pidgy, so get ready. If we lose a wicket you're in.'

'I either bat first or last, mate,' replied McGrath. 'I don't bat in the middle.'

● LLOYD'S LOW BLOW

The 1974-75 Ashes series became known as the Bouncer War, as both sides tried to intimidate one another with their fastest bowlers. Unfortunately for England, Australia boasted the menacing pair of Dennis Lillee and Jeff Thomson, both considerably faster and more fearsome than any of their opposite numbers.

It was an unusual time for Bumble to start looking for the penny he'd lost.

At Perth, traditionally the fastest track in Australia, David Lloyd had survived a Thomson onslaught to make 49 and declared after his innings that he could play the Aussie paceman 'with my prick'. Sadly for Lloyd, his bold statement was put to the test in the second innings. He'd reached 17 when Thomson sent in a venomous delivery which struck Lloyd in what the *Daily Telegraph* politely described as his groin, but what we all know was his meat and two veg.

The likeable Lancastrian crumpled into a heap, but has since made something of an after-dinner circuit routine out of the incident. He says: 'They got me to my feet and I said, "Can you take the pain away and leave the swelling?" Everything that should have been on the inside of this pink plastic box I was wearing for protection had found its way to the outside. The plastic had split and then snapped shut. I didn't need a doctor, I needed a welder.'

● SARKY SECURITY

As is now no doubt clear from this chapter, absolutely nobody is immune to the power of Ashes Fever – and that includes the Lord's security guards. When Sebastian Coe arrived to pick up his ticket from the Grace Gates for an Ashes Test recently, he was turned away and told to try the North Gate instead.

'No, I was definitely told the Grace Gates,' insisted Coe. 'Surely, you recognise me? I'm Sebastian Coe, the double Olympic gold medallist and world record breaker in the 800m, 1500m and the mile.'

'Well, I wouldn't know about that, Sir,' replied the official. 'But if you really are Sebastian Coe, it shouldn't take you long to run round to the North Gate.'

MY FAVOURITE ASHES MOMENT

ENGLAND BOWLER DARREN GOUGH

'Personally, getting an Ashes hat-trick was a huge thing. I had been part of Shane Warne's hat-trick in 1994-95, then in 1999 at Sydney, it was my turn. I think I got three wickets in that Test match and I didn't mean to bowl any one of them three balls!

'It had been a long tour as usual, I'd bowled a lot of overs and I was tired. Most people had left the ground, I think, including many of my family and friends, so a lot of people actually missed it. It was a great thing for me, especially at Sydney, which has to go down as one of my favourite grounds – it's similar to Lord's in terms of what it's all about and I got a five-for there, a hat-trick and a fifty.

'The Australians took to me and they always made out as if I'm one of them, but I just thought: "No I'm not, mate. I'm as English as they come." I consider it a compliment, though, to the way I play, especially because the teams I played against in the nineties were so good, so it's nice to come out of it with some praise.

'Another great moment was in 1997 at Edgbaston when we beat them in the first Test, but it was false hope really, because we didn't go on to win the series. It was an amazing first morning. At one point, I bowled Greg Blewett out with a no-ball. I said to everyone: "Oh, don't worry. I'll get him out next ball." And he edged the next one to Nasser Hussain at third slip!

'The other one, and probably my favourite moment, was Melbourne in 1998-99. Australia needed 175 to win and it was an amazing effort from us [the hosts had been 130 for three at one stage]. Dean Headley took six wickets in the second innings and I got Glenn McGrath LBW [to win it and bowl them out for 162], but me and Dean probably bowled for about two hours unchanged – we couldn't come off at that point. We ended up winning the game and I'll never forget it. You can probably remember the image of me picking the stump up – it was an amazing Test match win for England against all odds.'

Goughie always put his hand up to ask the umpire a question.

CHAPTER TWO

THE GREATEST ASHES SLEDGES

An Ashes Test match without sledging is like a British politician without a dodgy expenses claim – it just wouldn't be right. With the Aussies having pioneered the use of verbals, it wasn't long before the English caught on and then the fun really started. Here, we present the best exchanges between England and Australia players and, occasionally, spectators. Because, let's face it, for all the drama and excitement of the actual cricket, this is what it's really all about, isn't it?

● SIGN OF THE TIMES

England's Ken Farnes was bowling to Stan McCabe, who was in fine fettle and blasted him for six. A frustrated Farnes turned to Bill O'Reilly at the non-striker's end: 'What can I bowl to him? What can I do next?'

'Well, you could run down and get his autograph.'

● WHO'S THE WALLY NOW?

Australia wicketkeeper Wally Grout was batting well at Headingley and helping his side build a commanding first-innings lead when he had a visit from Fred Trueman, who was fielding at slip. Looking down at the pitch, Trueman said: 'I wouldn't like to be you fellows batting on this in the second innings.'

'The way you are bowling, Freddie, we won't have to,' replied Grout.

● SCATHING SKIPPERS

England captain Michael Vaughan arrived at the wicket and was met with a volley of abuse from his opposite number Ricky Ponting.

Vaughan: 'Get back to the slips, Ponting. Who do you think you are? Steve Waugh?'

● PASSPORT POP

In what must be the first of its kind, Australia captain Mark Taylor was sledged before he had even technically arrived in the UK for an Ashes tour. Upon handing over his passport at Heathrow immigration, an official said: 'Oh, Mark Taylor, eh? The Australian captain?'

Taylor nodded.

'Ahhh,' said the official. 'But for how long?'

● AN ILLEGITIMATE DEBATE

In the heat of the Bodyline battle, England captain Douglas Jardine paid a visit to the Australia dressing room and was met at the door by Vic Richardson. 'I would like to speak to [Australia Captain Bill] Woodfull,' said Jardine. 'One of your men called Larwood a bastard. I want an immediate apology.'

'Hey,' called out Richardson to the dressing room. 'Which of you bastards called Larwood a bastard instead of Jardine?'

● POETRY IN SLOW MOTION

Australia batsman Herbie Collins spent a seemingly endless five hours making 40 in the 1921 Old Trafford Test, trying the patience of everyone concerned. One of the spectators called out to England captain Lionel Tennyson, grandson of the famous poet: 'Hey Tennyson, read him some of thy granddad's poems!'

'He has done,' replied England fielder Cecil Parkin. 'And the beggar's been asleep for hours!'

● AN UGLY EXCHANGE

England opening batsman Andrew Sandham was fielding on the boundary next to the famous SCG Hill in the 1924-25 Ashes. One spectator persistently asked him to move: 'Sandy, ask your skipper to send out someone else, you're too ugly!'

Eventually, England captain Arthur Gilligan took pity on Sandham and replaced him with Patsy Hendren, but before Hendren had even strolled halfway to the boundary, the spectator bellowed: 'Send back Sandham!'

Patsy Hendren: too ugly to smile.

● A BRIDGE TOO FAR

When Fred Trueman was touring Australia, he became a little fed up of the proud Sydney locals constantly asking him and his teammates: 'What do you think of our bridge?'

After doing a little research, Trueman was ready when the question was asked again later that evening: 'What do I think of your bridge? It was built in Yorkshire by a firm called Dorman Long – and it isn't paid for yet!'

● HOLLIES' HUMOUR

England and Warwickshire's Eric Hollies was enduring a tough spell at the hands of two Australia batsmen. One of them attempted to undermine him further by asking: 'Don't they bury their dead in Birmingham?'

'No,' replied Hollies. 'We stuff them and mark them "Export Only."'

● MISSING IN ACTION

England's batsmen suffered countless problems trying to deal with Shane Warne, and Dean Headley was no exception: 'I remember trying to work out how to play against Shane Warne and not doing very well. Then Ramprakash and Thorpe told me not to just play back, as Bumble [coach David Lloyd] had been saying. If it spins and you don't know which way it's going, then imagine it's going straight on. Therefore you play for your stumps and, if it does spin, you'll miss it anyway.

'I decided to do this and I remember playing about twelve balls on the trot at Sydney where I prodded, gave it a chance to turn, and played and missed. Mark Waugh looked at me from silly mid-off and said: "Will you f**king hit it, you retard?"

'So I turned round to wicketkeeper Ian Healy and said: "I think he's confusing me with Don Bradman."'

● WARNE TAKES THE HONOURS

Whenever Warne batted he received plenty of abuse from England, including some sharp words from Paul Collingwood at the 2006-07 Sydney Test. Collingwood, who had famously played only in the final 2005 Ashes Test but still received an MBE like the rest of the team, was not expecting this reply from Warne: 'You got an MBE, right? For scoring seven at The Oval? That's embarrassing.'

● TAKING THE MICHAEL

Mike Atherton was on his first Ashes tour when he seemed to have been caught behind by Ian Healy. But, despite the loud appeals, the Englishman stood his ground and was given not out. At the end of the over, Healy walked past Atherton and hissed: 'You're a f**king cheat!'

'When in Rome, dear boy ...' Atherton replied.

● HITTING THE RIGHT KEY

Atherton was left speechless, however, when he played and missed once too often for Merv Hughes's liking: 'I'll bowl you a f**king piano, you Pommie poof,' said the Australian. 'Let's see if you can play that.'

● THE NAME GAME

Jimmy Anderson tried to get under the skin of Aussie batsman Mike Hussey during the opening Ashes Test at Brisbane in 2010-11. Throughout Hussey's innings, Anderson kept calling him Dave, which is the name of the batsman's non-Test playing brother. It didn't work, as 'Dave' made 195.

● INSTANT KARMA

Anderson and Mitchell Johnson had several run-ins during that series. At Perth, Johnson was batting at the non-striker's end and, as Anderson walked back to his mark, the pair were involved in an exchange that finished with the Australian asking: 'Why are you chirping now, mate, not getting wickets?'

Anderson promptly steamed in, clean-bowled Ryan Harris and, almost ignoring his celebrating teammates, called out 'Hey Mitch!' and placed a finger over his lips.

● FAMILY MISFORTUNE

Tailender Jimmy Ormond arrived at the crease at The Oval in 2001 with England in trouble – pretty soon, he was in the verbal firing line.

'What the f**k are you doing out here?' asked Mark Waugh at slip. 'Surely you're not good enough to play for England?'

'Maybe not,' replied Ormond, 'But at least I'm the best player in my family.'

As a postscript to this classic, Aussie bowler Jason Gillespie was in the field at the time and remembers the moment only too well. 'Adam Gilchrist was behind the stumps and he had to excuse himself and walk away because he was laughing too hard. Justin Langer was laughing at short leg and Shane Warne couldn't bowl because he was too busy giggling. We were all laughing our heads off. Even Mark was laughing. He thought it was a great comeback to a sledge.'

● GETTING HIS PHIL

Phil Tufnell wheeled away in delight after bowling Craig McDermott in the 1990-91 Perth Test, but he was soon quietened by the Australian's departing jibe: 'You've got to bat on this in a minute, Tufnell. Hospital food suit you?'

● HEADING FOR TROUBLE

Dennis Lillee bowled a bouncer at Derek Randall, who was busy compiling the innings of his life in the 1977 Centenary Test.

'It's no good hitting me there, mate,' Randall told Lillee. 'There's nothing to damage.'

Derek Randall's limbo cricket idea never really took off.

● TRIGGER HAPPY

Aussie paceman Paul Reiffel was a little too fired up during an Ashes warm-up match. He was struggling to dismiss a tailender so bellowed: 'You're the worst batsman I've ever seen.'

'I'm number eleven,' replied the batsman. 'What did you expect?'

● SEE NO EVIL, HEAR NO EVIL

When England were playing against Victoria and Phil Tufnell's huge appeal against Dean Jones was turned down, there was nothing left to do but sledge the umpire.

'Are you bloody blind?' said Tuffers to the official as he walked past him.

'I beg your pardon?' replied the umpire.

'Are you f**king deaf as well?'

● WARM WELCOME

Fred Trueman once greeted an incoming Australia batsman out of the pavilion at Lord's. As the tourist turned to close the gate, Trueman said: 'Don't bother shutting it. You'll be back soon.'

● OFF-HAND COMMENT

England spinner 'Deadly' Derek Underwood was struck a painful blow on the hand while batting in Australia. Concerned Australia captain Ian Chappell ran up to Underwood as he flung off his batting gloves: 'How's the hand?' enquired Chappell. 'Which one was it?'

'It was my right,' replied Underwood.

'Oh, that's a shame,' said Chappell. 'We were aiming for the left.'

● REVERSE PSYCHOLOGY

Australia were struggling on 84 for five at Melbourne in 2006-07 when all-rounder Andrew Symonds came in to bat. When he reached the crease, England's Kevin Pietersen announced: 'Here comes the specialist fielder.'

Symonds clearly used that as inspiration as he went on to score 156.

● SILENT SLEDGING

England decided against sledging Australia's Steve Waugh in the 1997 series, believing he responded well to all the jibes and insults. Unfortunately, Waugh soon twigged the rather cunning plan: 'Oh, I get it. Nobody's talking to Steve. OK! I'll talk to me f**king self!'

And he did. For four hours in the first innings for 108, and another three in the second for 116.

● BORED BORDER

Angus Fraser was thrilled at making Allan Border play and miss in that same series and made some sarcastic remarks to the Aussie captain.

'I've faced bigger, uglier bowlers than you, mate,' replied Border. 'Now f**k off and bowl the next one.'

● NATURAL BORN BATSMAN

David Hookes was batting for Australia in the Centenary Test at Melbourne in 1977 when England's resident South African Tony Greig eyed an opportunity to unsettle the 21-year-old.

'When are your balls going to drop, sonny?' asked Greig.

'I don't know, but at least I'm playing cricket for my own country,' replied Hookes.

● KEEPER'S CAPER

Aussie wicketkeeper Tim Zoehrer had had enough of England's Phil Edmonds' sledging and decided to hit back at the spinner, who was married to famous author Frances.

'At least I have an identity,' said Zoehrer. 'You're only Frances Edmonds' husband.'

● TICKETS PLEASE

Nasser Hussain was shining with the bat in the 1997 Edgbaston Test when substitute fielder Justin Langer decided to lend him his tuppence worth of verbals.

'Look, I don't mind the others chirping at me, but you're just the bus driver of this team,' snapped Hussain. 'So you get back on the bus and get ready to drive it back to the hotel this evening.'

● WHO ATE ALL THE PIES?

Derek Randall arrived at the wicket on the second day of the 1978 Boxing Day Test at Melbourne and sized up (literally) the situation. He turned to burly wicketkeeper John Maclean and said: 'I bet Santa didn't come to thy house. Tha's eaten all the mince pies, tha fat booger!'

● BEEFY'S BANTER

During one Test match, Australia wicketkeeper Rod Marsh welcomed Ian Botham to the wicket by asking: 'So how's your wife and my kids?'

Botham's response?

'The wife's fine, but the kids are retarded.'

● HUSSAIN'S HOOTER, PART 1

In a tour match at Essex, Nasser Hussain was batting and wicketkeeper Ian Healy asked his colleague Stuart Law to place himself 'right under Nasser's nose'.

Law started walking towards the boundary and kept going, before yelling to Healy: 'F**k me! The ground's not big enough, mate!'

● HUSSAIN'S HOOTER, PART 2

On another occasion, captain Steve Waugh was rearranging his field and decided Ricky Ponting should go at silly point to distract the England batsman.

'I want you right under Nasser's nose,' said Waugh, neatly setting up his teammates for an easy gag. Healy saw the open goal and duly obliged: 'That would be anywhere inside a three-mile radius!'

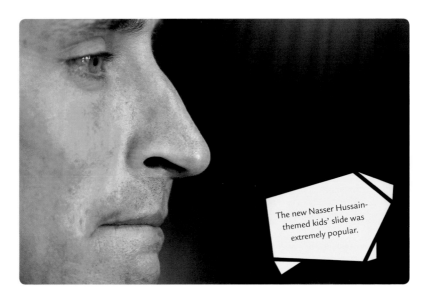

The new Nasser Hussain-themed kids' slide was extremely popular.

● WHAT ARE YOU TALKING ABOUT, WILLIS?

We all know about Phil Tufnell's experience at the hands of the Aussie fan who wanted to borrow the Englishman's brain to help him build an idiot (*see* England's Ashes Heroes). And he certainly wasn't alone in taking abuse from over-enthusiastic Australians, with Bob Willis also suffering these two corkers from spectators on the Hill at the SCG: 'Hey, Willis! I didn't know they stacked sh*t that high!'

'You take ugly pills? You must be hooked on them!'

● COOKING UP A TREAT

Australia opener Matthew Hayden published a book about his hobby of cooking, and received an earful from a spectator during an Ashes warm-up in England: 'Hayden, you're sh*t and so is your chicken casserole!'

● A THIRST FOR SLEDGING

When England batsman Robin Smith had the nerve to ask for some water during an innings, Aussie captain Allan Border yelled: 'What do you think this is, a f**king tea party?' 'No, you can't have a f**king glass of water. You can f**king wait like the rest of us.'

● FREDDIE'S FAUX PAS

In the closing stages of day two of the 2006-07 Adelaide Test, after England had made more than 500, Ricky Ponting opted to bat himself rather than send in a nightwatchman.

'I wouldn't like to be you if you get out here,' said England captain Andrew Flintoff.

'I wouldn't like to be you if we win from here, mate,' replied Ponting's partner Matthew Hayden. And, of course, they won.

● LAUGHING LILLEE

England began their 1994-95 Ashes tour with a warm-up match against an Australian Cricket Board XI, which featured former legends including Jeff Thomson, Rod Marsh and Dennis Lillee.

When England's rotund batsman Mike Gatting took strike against Lillee, the bowler began his run up before stopping and yelling: 'Move out of the way, Gatt. I can't see the stumps!'

MY FAVOURITE ASHES MOMENT

AUSTRALIA BOWLER
AND YORKSHIRE COACH
JASON GILLESPIE

'I was fortunate enough to be a member of an Ashes-winning side on a few occasions and they're obviously special moments, but I suppose the fact I was a young lad just starting out on my international journey meant that winning the Ashes on my first tour in 1997 was the most special.

'We lost the first Test, which I missed because I was injured, and Mark Taylor had been under pressure. He'd had a slump in form and the media were all over him. He got a hundred in that match, but we were still under pressure. We chipped away and slowly got ourselves back into the series and did really well.

'I took seven for 37 at Headingley [to put Australia 2-1 up], which was a nice personal moment and fortunately we won the game. I remember the Canberra Raiders rugby league side came into our dressing room for a drink after the game too, so that was another memorable moment.

'We wrapped up the Ashes at Trent Bridge where I didn't have a particularly good game or do anything outstanding, but to win the Ashes on my first England tour was so special. I remember we had a good celebration in the dressing rooms. It was nothing out of control but, because I was a young lad and relatively new to the team, it still stands out for me. I remember sitting there with all the legends of the game around me – guys I grew up idolising like Ian Healy, Steve Waugh, Taylor, Warnie, McGrath – and being able to share the moment with those guys was pretty special. In those early days, I just pinched myself and realised how lucky I was to be involved with the Australia cricket team.'

Gillespie wanted to make sure that Robert Croft definitely knew he was out.

CHAPTER THREE

CLOSE OF PLAY

The on-pitch action may have ended for the day, but the battle for the Ashes often continues in the dressing rooms, nearby bars and team hotels. This chapter focuses on the English and Australian off-pitch antics that sometimes go a long way to deciding the destination of the urn. And even if they didn't, it's still a good excuse to tell some funny, often boozy, stories.

● THE PERFECT TONIC

When England won the Ashes in 2005 and proceeded to go on the mother of all benders to celebrate, there were some dissenting voices claiming 'it wasn't cricket'. If it wasn't cricket, then how to explain what happened more than one hundred years earlier, when the teams' willingness to shrug off the pressures of playing by drinking was much more pronounced? At least the Class of 2005 waited until they had won the series.

That was certainly not the case with the 1893 Australia tour to England, which was considered particularly wild, with the tour manager at the time stating: 'It was impossible to keep some of them straight. One of them was altogether useless because of his drinking propensities. Some were in the habit of holding receptions in their rooms and would not go to bed until all hours.'

If that was bad, alcohol wasn't just confined to the evenings in the following tour in 1896, although on this occasion it was strictly medicinal. Aussie captain Harry Trott was known for his innovative approach and he noticed that one of his batsmen, teetotal Frank Iredale, was suffering with nerves. At least that was the case until Trott ordered him to drink a 'tonic' before he went out to bat. Remarkably, Iredale's form improved and he went on to become the tourists' leading century-maker of the tour.

The tonic? Brandy and soda.

● AL FRESCO DRINKING

Whether voluntary or not, Iredale was certainly not the last Ashes player to drink during a Test match. During England's Bodyline tour of Australia, the tourists wrapped up victory in the searing Brisbane heat aided and abetted by champagne. The bowlers in particular were struggling to cope and joint-manager Richard Palairet suggested half-a-dozen sips of bubbly might help them. It certainly did the trick as Harold Larwood and co. completed an English win.

And when England toured Australia in 1946-47, Denis Compton became an instant crowd favourite. According to captain Wally

Hammond, spectators would constantly call him over while he was fielding with the cry of 'Have one with us, Denis,' as they brandished glasses of beer towards him. Perhaps it was the heat, or maybe he was just thirsty, but Compton would actually often join the locals for a drink at the fall of a wicket.

'I think he limited himself to two a day,' said Hammond. 'One in the morning and one in the afternoon.'

BEHAVING UNCEREMONIOUSLY

Ashes tours usually require players to attend functions, often to meet dignitaries and exchange pleasantries with local figures. With these events usually taking place in the evenings or on rest days, players can sometimes be forgiven for not taking matters entirely seriously.

Australia's Ernie Jones was possibly the earliest exponent of this dignitary duelling when he met King Edward VII. Jones, a fast bowler known for his quick-witted remarks, was asked by the king if he had attended St Peter's College, Adelaide.

'Yes,' he replied. 'I drive the dust cart there every week.'

HOGG CAUGHT BY FINE LEG

The best royal moment of all undoubtedly belongs to Rodney Hogg, part of the 1981 Aussie touring squad. Although Dennis Lillee can give him a decent run for his money when he flaunted tradition in 1972 by greeting both the Queen and the Duke of Edinburgh at Buckingham Palace by replacing the formal 'How do you do, ma'am/sir' with a more relaxed 'G'day', Hogg's observation still takes the prize.

Both England and Australia were being introduced to the Queen and Prince Philip during the lunch interval at Lord's. As the royal couple were meeting the England players, Hogg desperately tried to attract his colleague Geoff Lawson's attention. Lawson (nicknamed Henry) takes up the story: 'After several attempts at ignoring him,

I finally gave in and asked what the problem was. He simply pointed towards the Queen and said in a voice that could have been heard at Buckingham Palace, "Jeez, Henry. She hasn't got bad legs for an old sheila, has she?" I nearly fainted.'

● LEN-DING A HELPING HAND

Gloating is said to be most unbecoming, but it's also very funny, as proved by Len Hutton, who captained England to an Ashes victory in Australia in 1954-55.

With the urn in the bag and England 3-1 up in the series, Hutton strode through a Hobart hotel's lounge where he encountered four members of the Australia team – Richie Benaud, Alan Davidson, Neil Harvey and Les Favell. Unable to resist the temptation, Hutton offered each of the players an hour's free nets coaching before the final Test.

● THE LOVING CUP OF VICTORY

One would imagine that the Test match that created the Ashes would have seen animosity between the teams at its peak. In fact, despite the best efforts of W.G.Grace to push the limits of gamesmanship, when Australia wrapped up a famous victory by dismissing England for 77 in the 1882 Oval Test, both teams celebrated together in the Australians' dressing room.

Victorious Tom Horan recalled in the *Australasian*: 'Never shall I forget the wild excitement of the moment ... how not only the Australians but Englishmen rushed into our dressing room and shook hands with us all around; how they mingled with champagne, seltzer and lemons and passed the drink round like a loving cup.'

● LOST IN TRANSLATION

Aussie leg spinner Arthur Mailey was invited to the Royal Box during the 1921 Lord's Test. Feeling somewhat fatigued from his efforts – he'd bowled 39 overs and taken six wickets in the match – and miffed at being ignored by the princess next to whom he was seated, he remarked in her general direction: 'I'm a little stiff from bowling.'

'Oh is that where you're from?' replied the royal. 'I was wondering.'

● YOU'RE WELCOME

Johnny Douglas was the captain of the touring England team in 1911-12, after Pelham Warner fell ill, and his 'welcome' speech at Melbourne Town Hall is the stuff of legend.

The former Olympic boxer and amateur footballer stood up, cleared his throat and said no more and no less than the following: 'I hate speeches. As Bob Fitzsimmons once said: "I ain't no bloomin' orator, but I'll fight any man in this blinkin' country!"'

Needless to say, he wasn't the most popular touring captain.

● CLIMBING TO THE EVANS

While it may not be on a par with Gower's Tiger Moth stunt, England wicketkeeper Godfrey Evans also hit the heights in Australia.

Following the Ashes-clinching victory at Adelaide in 1954-55, the England team were celebrating hard at the team hotel. Champagne corks were popping, glasses were being drained and the players were, well ... drunk.

Evans was bet £100 that he could not scale a 20-foot column in the hotel and touch the ceiling. To the amazement of all watching, the keeper sprang up the column with all the agility of a monkey and reached the ceiling in no time. He never kept the money, though, as he offered double or quits to his challenger, who also managed to perform the feat.

● KEEPING THEM PEELED

Years earlier, several England players didn't even bother waiting until the end of the Test match for their night out.

Australia were 113 for two, requiring only 64 more runs for victory going into the final day of the first Test of the 1894-95 series in Sydney. With the result a formality, some of the England team, including spinner Bobby Peel, took in a few of the city's nightspots and were feeling the pinch the following morning.

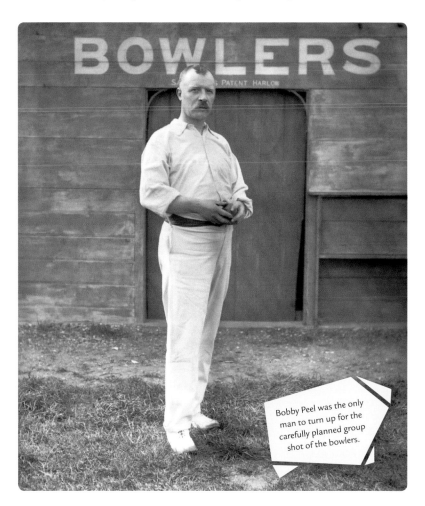

Bobby Peel was the only man to turn up for the carefully planned group shot of the bowlers.

When they arrived back at the ground, they found conditions had changed dramatically as overnight rain had turned the uncovered pitch into an unpredictable 'sticky dog', which meant England still had a chance of an unlikely victory.

England skipper Andrew Stoddart realised he had to take immediate action to revive his players, as much as his team's chances, so he threw Peel into a cold shower to shake off the effects of the previous night. Amazingly, it worked, as Peel took five Australia wickets to help England sneak home by 10 runs as the home side collapsed from 158 for five to 166 all out.

● RICHIE AT THE DOUBLE

Peel's was one of many Ashes hangovers, as drinking became a right of passage for every young, impressionable cricketer on an Ashes tour – even strait-laced Richie Benaud wasn't spared.

On his first tour of England in 1953, Benaud had not enjoyed a good opening Test at Trent Bridge with the bat, being dismissed for 3 and 0 ahead of the rest day. The team attended a party in Nottingham that evening at which Lindsay Hassett was drinking a scotch while his teammate Benaud sipped on an orange juice.

Hassett was unimpressed with Benaud's choice and implored him to have a proper drink, but the spinner was reluctant as the Test match was still ongoing. Eventually Hassett wore Benaud down and convinced him to have a taste of whisky, which the young spinner declared to be 'tasteless'.

'I had eleven doubles and a treble,' says Benaud. 'And, when I got back to the hotel, the bed dumped me on the floor. I had a rugged night.'

Worse was to come for Benaud, as the team were due to be hosted by the Duke of Portland the following morning. Benaud boarded the team bus feeling wretched and plotting to sit near the driver so he could make him stop if the worst were to happen. But no sooner had he got on board than someone called out: 'Good morning, Richie.' It was the voice of Sir Don Bradman, seated next to Lady Bradman. 'So I sat on that bus with my teeth clenched for eighteen miles,' admits Benaud. 'It was the most agonising trip I've ever gone through.'

● BOAT PARTY

It's hard to imagine what kind of damage both England and Australia might do on an eight-week voyage these days but, in 1921, the two teams sailed from Sydney to Portsmouth shortly after Australia had whitewashed England for the first time. And, according to Aussie Charles Macartney, a rather spiffing time was had by all: 'Warren Bardsley was the champion at quoits [don't ask, it's essentially posh hoopla]. Makepeace as a pirate, Hendren as Tarzan of the Apes and Fender as Rasputin excelled at the fancy dress ball. Australians were well represented, too, with Bardsley as a mixture of W.G.Grace and the Ancient Mariner, Johnny Taylor as a Chinese mandarin, and myself as a young lady.'

The tabloids would have had a field day.

● GENTLE JIM

Not everyone lived up to the high standards set by the partying players on that barmy boat bash. When England retained the Ashes at Old Trafford in 1956, one man in particular had cause to celebrate and celebrate hard – Flintoff style.

Jim Laker took an astonishing 19 wickets in the match to single-handedly bowl England to victory, a performance unmatched in any Test before or since, or indeed in any first-class game in history. Yet his post-match antics were slightly lower-profile than the England all-rounder's nearly 50 years later.

Having stayed at the ground for 'congratulations all round and photographs', Laker then conducted a series of newspaper, radio and television interviews before spending 30 minutes signing autographs.

He then had to drive back to London for another game the next day (this was long before the concept of central contracts or resting weary bowlers had been invented). On the way, he stopped in a pub near Lichfield.

'My celebration dinner consisted of a bottle of beer and a sandwich,' he wrote in his autobiography. 'I sat in the corner of a crowded bar for 15 minutes while everyone talked of the Test match. No one spotted me. Beyond asking how far I had to go, the landlord said nothing.'

All of which is a far cry from allegedly urinating in the prime minister's garden.

● MARSH MAKES MERRY

Laker's quiet contemplation of his monumental achievement was a world away from Rod Marsh's shenanigans in 1972 for much less. The Australian hit the winning run in the final Test at The Oval to earn the tourists a draw in the series, but England still retained the Ashes.

That didn't stop Marsh cartwheeling off the pitch and into the dressing room before mounting a table and launching into the first rendition of what would become the Australia cricket team's official victory song, 'Under the Southern Cross':

Under the Southern Cross I stand
A sprig of wattle in my hand
A native of my native land
Australia, you f**king beauty!

And that was pretty much the last thing Marsh would remember about that evening.

● HAIR TO THE THRONE

Jason Gillespie recalls another amusing contretemps between the Queen and one of her loyal subjects: 'I met the Queen on each of my three Ashes tours, which was always nice. I remember in 2001, I was standing not too far away from Colin Miller and he had different-coloured hair [it was bright blue at the time]. The Queen sort of looked at him and in not so many words said: "What the heck is that?" and they had a bit of a laugh together. It was a nice moment.'

It was the morning after Colin Miller's night out with Freddie Flintoff.

● RANDALL'S RANDOMNESS, PART 1

Not every night following a tough day's play needs to end with a lengthy drinking session – just ask England's Derek Randall.

After a hard day in the field during an Adelaide Test, Randall returned to the team hotel and decided to run a bath. As he paced around the room wrapped in his towel waiting for the tub to fill,

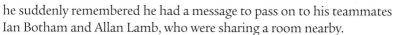

he suddenly remembered he had a message to pass on to his teammates Ian Botham and Allan Lamb, who were sharing a room nearby.

He nipped out to visit them and they invited him in for a cup of Earl Grey tea and a chat. As he returned to his room, Randall realised he had locked himself out.

Ordinary folk dressed in just a towel would have asked Botham or Lamb to help them, but Randall does not fall under the ordinary folk umbrella. He simply strolled down to the Adelaide Hilton reception for a replacement key, but as he arrived downstairs there was a commotion.

Guests dressed in black tie who were attending a hotel function were running out of the dining area sopping wet. While Randall, still in just his towel, waited for a new key at reception, he casually enquired what all the fuss was about.

'Well,' said the receptionist. 'Some stupid dick has left their bath water running and flooded the dining area!'

● RANDALL'S RANDOMNESS, PART 2

The Adelaide Test in 1982-83 was certainly an eventful one for Randall – but not with the bat, with which he made just 0 and 17. He trumped his flooding of the Adelaide Hilton with a performance of extraordinary authenticity outside a red light district bar that perhaps should have seen him nominated for an Oscar.

According to an after-dinner circuit story which has now been doing the rounds for years, Randall and Botham had a bet that if he went outside the bar to tout for business he wouldn't get picked up. Somehow, most probably thanks to the generosity of a punter in the bar, Randall was soon dressed in a tight leather skirt and carrying a handbag outside the watering hole.

The England players inside gathered at the window to watch the spectacle and, to their amazement, their colleague was soon seen being invited into a car which then drove off. Within a few minutes a scruffy Randall returned to the bar and pocketed Botham's money before explaining that he was forced to use his handbag to fend off the amorous advances of the car's driver.

● A NAKED NET

On first sight, a story about a naked cricketer in their hotel room at 6am is probably not going to be flattering for the person in question. Except Geoff Marsh wasn't completely naked – he was wearing a helmet, batting gloves and holding his, er, bat while looking in the mirror. Still not great, is it?

This was the sight that greeted David Boon when he opened one eye very early on the first morning of the first Ashes Test at Headingley in 1989. Marsh was rehearsing his forward defensive in front of the mirror as the adrenalin and nerves of the Ashes ensured he couldn't sleep.

Unfortunately, the extra practice didn't pay off – Marsh was first man out that morning for 16. The sight clearly didn't help Boon, either, as he fell for 9 – Australia lost just one other wicket that day.

● ANOTHER VICTORY SONG

Australia went on to win that series which had been preceded by England's 1986-87 Ashes victory – their last on Australian soil for 24 years. But, as luck would have it, their celebration party after tying up the series with a win in Melbourne was a fitting way to enter such a dry era.

Elton John had been following the team around Australia for most of the tour and he joined the team in the dressing room after the game. 'He got champagne thrown all over one of his silk suits which had cost him about five grand,' said victorious captain Mike Gatting. 'It was great having a legend like him in the dressing room.'

David Gower, who like Ian Botham was friendly with the singer, said: 'Elton had become our number one groupie. He was not supposed to be on tour in Australia when we were there, but he had to have an operation on his throat, so he decided to stay. He's not short of a bob or two, but he is a very generous soul and he looked after us.'

● DOMESTIC LEAVES FRED MAJESTIC

Sometimes it's not the all-night partying which can prove troubling for players on the night before a match, as Fred Trueman found out during the 1961 Headingley Test. In fact, Yorkshire's finest had been involved in a blazing row with his wife and was kicked out of his house, meaning he spent all night outside Headingley trying to sleep in his car.

He managed to use the whole situation to his advantage the next day when he ran through the Aussies for the second time in the match, taking five wickets in just 24 balls for no runs to finish with match figures of 11 for 88. Have some of that, Mrs Trueman.

Trueman's pre-match warm-up routine was legendary.

● BEEFY ON BRAND-Y

The successful 1986-87 tour was as exciting for the England players off the pitch as it was on it, if Ian Botham's account of one night out is anything to go by.

Beefy was invited to a party at the headquarters of the White Crusader America's Cup sailing team the night before a warm-up match against Western Australia, a special fixture to mark the Aussies defending the America's Cup.

Alongside Mike Gatting, John Emburey, Allan Lamb, David Gower and Chris Broad, Botham didn't hold back on the drinks front: 'It turned out to be a fantastic night,' he writes in his autobiography. 'I had tucked into a bottle of brandy and when it was time to leave I found I could hardly put one foot in front of the other.'

Beefy had to be carried out and woke up the next morning with 'one of the biggest hangovers of my life', which, if said by most of us, wouldn't really mean much. But, coming from Botham, really must be put into context. It was colossal.

Botham employed every delaying tactic he could to avoid having to bat that morning, conspiring with physio Lawrie Brown to come up with a series of niggles and pains. Eventually, with England 69 for six, Botham was forced to enter the fray: 'Halfway out to the wicket I got the shock of my life when someone tapped me on the shoulder. For obvious reasons, the identity of the twelfth man remains a mystery to me. I do recall exactly what he said, however. "Beefy... I think you might need this." He was holding my bat in his hands.'

● GRIN AND BEAR IT

By the end of a tour, if you've managed to survive unscathed from fearsome opposition bowlers and any number of wild nights out, it's safe to assume you're going to make it home in one piece. But this almost wasn't the case for Aussie bowler Sid Emery, who so nearly fell at the final hurdle on the way back from the 1912 Ashes.

The players were travelling on a train near Minneapolis, USA, when it stopped in a small town called Theodore. From his window, Emery spotted a bear tied to a post. He grabbed his camera and stepped down from the train to take a picture.

Bravely, or foolishly, venturing close to the animal while adjusting the focus on his machine, Emery suddenly came under attack from the bear and fell in shock. With the cricketer at his mercy, the bear swiped at Emery with its paw, only for the bowler to roll out of the animal's reach at the last possible moment and run back to the train in fear for his life.

● PARKING THE BUS

England were 3-0 down in the 2002-03 Ashes when they broke for a couple of one-day internationals in which they didn't fare much better. But all-rounder Ronnie Irani was determined to have a drink with the Australians after the game to try to humanise the people who were giving England such a torrid time.

'After a game at the SCG,' says Irani, 'I was with Owais Shah and Marcus Trescothick and a few young lads, and I was off to the Aussie dressing room – Nasser Hussain and Duncan Fletcher did not encourage mixing with the Aussies; they wanted us to keep our distance. I thought it was better to look them in the eye and realise they were only human. The young lads followed me into the Aussies' dressing room and they loved it. Two hours later, Alec Stewart told us Nasser and Fletcher had taken the team bus back.

'I got back to the hotel and Nasser was at the bar. He called out to me: "Sucking up to the Aussies, are you? Kissing the Aussies' arses, are you?" I said: "No, not at all, I know Steve Waugh and Mark Waugh quite well, you know."

'Nasser didn't seem to like mixing with anybody during a Test series. When Mike Atherton was captain, he also didn't appear to be keen on socialising with the opposition, and I think that cost England when Atherton and Hussain were in charge for that period. Everyone's different, but I think that would have done the players a world of good. Under Michael Vaughan's captaincy, the players mixed with each other and they took them on, on a level playing field rather than go the other way. I believe that was to England's advantage.'

● BAD SANTA

When morale was low in the England camp – as it often was during Ashes contests in the nineties – they could always rely on Darren Gough to lighten the mood.

On the 1998-99 tour, team spirit slumped to a new low after Australia A chased down 376 in 55 overs to defeat an England team, already 2-0 down in the Test series. Luckily, Gough, who wasn't playing in that game, was waiting in the dressing room to cheer everyone up.

'I was dressed as Santa Claus,' he says. 'The lads had been smacked all over the park by Aussie A, so I sat Angus Fraser on my knee and said: "Come here now, what do you want for Christmas, son?

Goughie's W.G.Grace impression always went down a storm.

I've got a big bag here, but the reason why this bag is so heavy is because I've just had to carry your bowling figures over from the score box!" Everybody was in hysterics for about twenty-five minutes. Gus was always miserable and took a bit of stick, but it relaxed everybody.'

It certainly did the trick as a week later England won the Boxing Day Test at Melbourne in a thrilling game.

● WINE AND CHEESE(BURGER) TASTING

Back in 1982-83, Ian Botham was the man who could always be relied upon to lighten the mood. On a rare night off, Botham hosted a party in his hotel room, which consisted of the team 'demolishing every bottle of booze we could lay our hands on'.

Beefy takes up the story: 'When we came round the next day (a day off I must add) we were rather taken aback to find the room was full of bits of uneaten cheeseburger. Somewhere along the line we had ordered up a couple of dozen from room service but had actually eaten none. They were everywhere. [Bob] Willis had one enmeshed in his hair and when I woke up, someone politely inquired: "Beefy, are you aware that there is a cheeseburger stuck in your ear?"'

● AUSTRALIA'S ASHES FLIGHTS TO ENGLAND: A SHORT HISTORY OF DRINKING

It all started on the way back from Australia's 1973 tour of the Caribbean when Doug Walters and Rod Marsh began speculating on how many beers they might be able to consume during the journey. Thirty hours later, there were no beers left on the plane and the pair had long since moved on to spirits, but the foundations of what would become Australian cricket's most sought-after record for the next two decades were laid.

Close of Play

When it came to carrying the beer, Lillee and Marsh took no chances.

Four years later, the Australia Ashes squad boarded its flight to London and, while there was very little talk of taking on the Poms for the urn, the plane was awash with speculation on who would win the inaugural Ashes drinking contest. A points system was created to reward drinks in different categories and sizes. Kim Hughes was an early pacesetter, but ran out of steam before Singapore, leaving Walters and Marsh to slug it out all the way to the UK.

As the plane touched down at Heathrow, Walters drained the contents of his 44th can of beer to take the title, with Marsh spitting feathers and claiming he'd matched his teammate drink for drink. Walters attributed his success to a steady pace, telling the *Weekend Australian Magazine*: 'I'm a sipper. I can sip all day and it doesn't have a great effect, but I can't put 'em down at a hundred miles an hour. I'm not a fast drinker.'

Marsh was hurt and, with no serious efforts made to take the record in 1981, had to wait six years for his chance to take revenge when he was part of the Aussie squad that travelled to the 1983 World Cup in England. But the wicketkeeper's attempt was sabotaged by Dennis Lillee, who wrote in his autobiography: 'I didn't want him watching the World Cup series on television in the drying-out ward of some London hospital.' And his plan to stop this happening? Well, plying Marsh with drink, of course. Lillee decided to have as many drinks as possible with Marsh the night before the flight and even managed to drink a few more at the airport before boarding – not that this deterred Marsh in any way. It simply made his task harder, but he rose to the challenge.

By the time the plane had started its descent into London, Marsh was struggling with his 43rd beer as excitement mounted in the cabin, mainly due to the captain having announced the record attempt. Feeling the pressure, and the excess alcohol at altitude no doubt, Marsh almost gave in, but Lillee – after a dramatic change of heart about the potential hospitalisation of his teammate – took matters into his own hands.

'The challenge had by now assumed the significance of winning an Ashes series,' he wrote. 'There would be no capitulation. We tilted Rodney's head back and literally force-fed him.' By the time he'd finished the record-breaking 45th can, Lillee recorded that Marsh was 'history. Drunk as a monkey. Full as a fowl.'

Whereas six years earlier, Walters – with 44 beers on board – had walked off the plane, Marsh, with that all-important 45th, had to be dressed and helped off the flight by Lillee and opening batsman Graeme Wood, and then loaded on to a luggage trolley to make it to customs.

There would be no such histrionics from David Boon in 1989. Although the Tasmanian, now an ICC match referee, has never officially talked about his successful attempt, others on that Ashes flight have, including Dean Jones, who sat next to Boon for the first half of the journey. Jones retired upstairs for a sleep after sharing 22 cans with Boon, only to wake up to a round of applause followed by the captain's announcement that Boon had shattered the record with 52 cans. Not only that, the batsman then walked off the flight with no baggage trolley required (other than for his bags).

One shudders to think what Boon's record would be if he had played a century ago when the Ashes 'flight' was an eight-week voyage on a ship ...

MY FAVOURITE ASHES MOMENT

ENGLAND BATSMAN AND ONE-DAY BATTING COACH GRAHAM THORPE

'My favourite memory as a kid was watching Botham play in 1981. I was 12 years old at the time and I can remember watching it on TV at our local cricket club – that memory stands out for me.

'My debut at Trent Bridge was an interesting one. Allan Border was captain and Merv Hughes delivered the first ball I faced and I had David Boon at short leg – these were pretty experienced campaigners and I was only 23 years old (although those moustaches weren't really for me!). I can remember copping quite a bit from them – they weren't particularly complimentary. That was when the *Sun* had their long microphones on the boundary edge and I think they recorded 40 f-words being aimed at me in the first five overs. But that was pretty expected at that time.

'I got a hundred against them in the second innings and, because of the type of side they had at that time, it was a proud moment if you scored a century against their attack. I played against the likes of Gillespie, McGrath and Warne and, later on in my career, Brett Lee. They were a pretty formidable attack. That was an exceptional side and they kept on developing throughout the decade I was up against them. Victories in my era were few and far between, so runs scored against them were valued and I was proud of those moments.

'I wouldn't say that century totally set me up as a player, but it certainly gave me an opportunity to get off and running and it gave me confidence, but it was just the beginning.

'The battles against Warne and McGrath really stand out for me as well. It was a great challenge. They went on to become great players and in the early battles against them, you knew they were very good, but they didn't have 500 wickets under their belts by then. Those battles were pretty special.'

Thorpe and Healy were global stars of the new mime cricket craze.

CHAPTER FOUR

FLASHPOINTS

Sometimes, cricket just isn't cricket – and this can occur quite often during the heat of the Ashes battle. This chapter celebrates, ahem, recalls those unsavoury incidents when events came close to spiralling out of control, as tempers flared both on and off the pitch. So let's try not to laugh, as we rubberneck some of the Ashes' most famous flashpoints.

● HILL RUNS OUT OF LUCK

If you think Ricky Ponting kicked up a fuss after being run out by Gary Pratt in 2005, it seemed positively good-natured compared to the stink caused by the run out of Clem Hill in the 1903-04 opening Test in Sydney.

Both run outs took place in similar circumstances, with Australia fighting back from precarious positions. In this Test, Hill was unbeaten on 51 and, alongside Victor Trumper, was threatening to bring Australia back into contention after conceding a hefty first-innings deficit of 292.

The pair had run four and, when an attempted run out had sailed past the stumps, opted for a fifth despite Hill having overrun his ground by some distance. He appeared to have completed the run just when the stumps were broken, but a unanimous England appeal was upheld by umpire Bob Crockett. Business as usual then. Or not.

England captain Pelham Warner wrote in his book *How We Recovered The Ashes*: 'Hill did not say a word in protest to Crockett, but the way in which he walked back to the pavilion could not possibly have left anyone in doubt as to what he himself thought of Crockett's ruling.'

As soon as Hill had reached the pavilion, a chorus of hissing and booing began to ring around the ground. When Warner went to the pavilion to attempt to remonstrate with the members, the noise only increased until the new batsman Monty Noble emerged. The pair sat down for a couple of minutes and, amid a cacophony of barracking, Warner informed Noble he would have to take his team off the pitch if it continued, but the Australian captain counselled against such a move.

Eventually, the protest subsided, but as soon as play resumed the din rocketed up a level and there were shouts of 'How much did you pay Crockett, Warner?' and 'Have you got your coffin ready, Crockett?'

It was an unsavoury incident, even by the occasionally wild standard of early Ashes Test matches, and Warner was shocked enough to write: 'People in England can have no conception of the yelling and hissing that went on that afternoon right up to the drawing of stumps; even such hardened Test match players as [George] Hirst and [Wilfred] Rhodes were upset.'

England eventually won the match and the series – one can only imagine the kind of things the rascals in the stands would have been screaming at Warner by then.

● A TALE OF TWO PONTINGS

Well it's the same Ponting actually. It's Australia's captain Ricky losing the plot on two occasions, but it's called poetic licence – OK, pedants? Anyway, it's fair to say that by late 2010, Ricky was having a hard time adjusting to the fact that England had become a competitive force again after nigh-on two decades in the Ashes doldrums.

And after winning at home in 2009, Andrew Strauss's side were looking in good shape to make it three out of four series wins by registering their first success Down Under since 1986-87. None of which was particularly helping Ponting's mood, which boiled over twice in the space of a few weeks.

After England had saved the first Test at Brisbane by batting Australia into submission, the first day of the second Test had started disastrously for the Aussies, who were 2 for three at one stage, with Ponting out first ball to James Anderson. They were eventually dismissed for 245, leaving England to survive an over before stumps. They duly did that, but when Strauss was walking to the pavilion he was confronted by an irate Ponting, who was complaining about Anderson's antics earlier in the day, when the bowler had clashed with Aussie wicketkeeper Brad Haddin – imagine that, a bowler aggressively intimidating a batsman! No wonder Ponting was so upset.

A few weeks later, in the Boxing Day Test at Melbourne, with the series all square at 1-1, Ponting was under intense pressure again after Australia had been dismissed for just 98 and England were piling on the runs for fun. The hosts thought they had made a breakthrough with an appeal for Kevin Pietersen being caught behind, but the Decision Review System showed otherwise and Ponting exploded. He spent several minutes rowing with umpires Alim Dar and Tony Hill as he briefly lost the plot. He was duly fined 40 per cent of his match fee and said afterwards: 'I was simply trying to seek clarification from the umpires regarding how the decision had been made after being referred to the third umpire. However, I would be unhappy if anyone thought I was being disrespectful towards the umpires, as this wasn't my intention.'

Yeah, arguing with both umpires for two minutes while wagging your finger at them, that's not disrespectful at all.

Ponting made sure that everyone on the pitch knew exactly where his friends and family were sitting.

● WHITE HOT SNOW

There was even less respect on display in the 1970-71 Test at Sydney as the already simmering tension between the teams reached boiling point – with serious repercussions.

England paceman John Snow had been striking fear into Australia's batsmen all series with his aggressive bowling, which was doing its job – he returned home with 31 wickets in his back pocket.

But the animosity between the teams rose to the surface again in the final Test when Snow struck Aussie tailender Terry Jenner. It was a brutal, short-pitched delivery which Jenner had tried to duck under, but the ball still rose up to strike him on the side of his skull. In a sickening moment, he immediately collapsed at the crease and a wave of hostility towards Snow and England broke out around the SCG.

When the bowler returned to his fielding position near the boundary, he was attacked by a spectator, who grabbed hold of his shirt and, when Snow managed to free himself, a cloud of beer cans and bottles rained down on him from the stands. Captain Ray Illingworth had seen enough and ordered his side from the field, the umpires followed, leaving just the two Australia batsmen in the middle.

This is how Brian Johnston reported the incident live on the BBC: 'A few moments ago Snow bowled a short ball that hit Jenner on the head. It knocked him down and he was taken off to tremendous boos. The result was another batsman came in and Snow finished the over ... Snow then came down to the hill below us here, beer cans were thrown in the area where he was fielding ... they bombarded him with beer cans. Illingworth came down with half his team, said something to Snow and he led them off the field. It's an unprecedented position this, England refusing to go on. I'm in despair that such a thing could happen in a Test match. Whosoever is wrong, it could be England, it could be Australia, but this shouldn't be really allowed to happen.'

Eventually, police were forced to enter the playing field and clear up all the debris that had been thrown by the crowd and Illingworth returned with his players. Jenner also bravely returned to help Australia carve out a first-innings lead, but England struck back to win the match and take the series and the urn for the first time in twelve years.

● BARMY BARNES BRINGS BOOS

It was nothing new for Australian crowds to 'get one on them', as my mother-in-law likes to say – they'd been doing it for years. In the 1911-12 Ashes Test at Melbourne, a seemingly innocuous act enraged the locals.

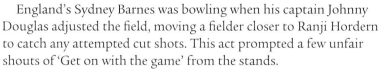

England's Sydney Barnes was bowling when his captain Johnny Douglas adjusted the field, moving a fielder closer to Ranji Hordern to catch any attempted cut shots. This act prompted a few unfair shouts of 'Get on with the game' from the stands.

Hordern described what happened next in his autobiography: 'Barnes, evidently strung up to concert pitch, suddenly lost his temper, foolishly threw the ball on the ground, facing the crowd and, folding his arms, stood glaring at them. Then he got what he was looking for: they howled at him just as heartily as they had previously cheered, and I am sorry to say hooting came from every part of the ground. As Barnes ran in to bowl, pandemonium broke loose. I stepped away from the wicket and sat on my bat, plainly asking the crowd to "shut up" and behave. This happened three times and I sat so long the last time that the hooting abated and the game proceeded. These are absolute facts: and wasn't it all so very wrong and so very silly?'

Sure was.

● METAL AS ANYTHING

The 1979-80 Ashes Test series wasn't actually an Ashes Test series. England did play Australia in three Test matches, but England's Test and County Cricket Board had deemed that three matches were not enough to constitute playing for the urn. Australia disagreed, but it mattered not and the Aussies' 3-0 series victory did not actually count for the Ashes. If only the ECB would now claim that all the Test matches between England and Australia between 1989 and 2003 were not for the Ashes, then modern English cricket history would look extremely healthy.

Despite the urn not being at stake, there was still plenty to play for – this was Australia v England after all. But it was a bizarre incident that caused controversy in the opening Test at Perth.

When Dennis Lillee came out to bat, everything seemed normal. But a strange noise was emerging from Lillee's bat whenever he made contact with the ball. This alerted the suspicions of the England players. Lillee had actually come out to the wicket with a metal bat and England captain Mike Brearley was far from happy, as he complained to the umpires that the bat was damaging the ball. There followed a ten-minute contretemps between Lillee, the umpires and Brearley, who refused to let his bowlers bowl at the Australian, or his bat.

Eventually, Aussie captain Greg Chappell sent out twelfth man Rodney Hogg with a selection of replacement bats, but Lillee dismissed his efforts, so the skipper himself had to come out to defuse the situation. Upon seeing Chappell in the middle, Lillee hurled the metal bat across the pitch in anger. And then play continued.

Lillee's metal bat ensured Border gave the world a rare glimpse of his teeth.

Lillee later admitted it had been a marketing ploy, as he was hoping to patent and sell the new aluminium bats, but they were banned almost as soon as the one he'd thrown had landed on the ground. He once joked: 'I now hold the record for throwing an aluminium bat the furthest in a Test match. And I know it will stand forever.'

Chappell actually knew about Lillee's intentions beforehand and tried to work them to his – and Australia's – advantage. His plan was to allow Lillee to use the bat for an over before ordering him to stop, thus sending him into a rage shortly before he was due to bowl at

England's opening pair, Geoff Boycott and Derek Randall. Luckily, Brearley did that job for Chappell and, suitably antagonised after being last man out a short while later, Lillee returned with the ball and removed both England openers for ducks.

● THE IKIN INCIDENT

If anyone tells you batsmen who don't walk are the scourge of the modern game, make sure you let them know that the game's greatest players of old were at it too.

W.G.Grace would never have dreamed of leaving his crease unless ordered to by the umpire and sometimes had to be physically forced off the pitch, while Don Bradman was involved in an infamous incident in the 1946-47 Ashes series.

It was the opening morning of the first post-war contest and Australia had lost a couple of early wickets, with Bradman's form looking patchy at best. Bill Voce looked to have dismissed the Don with a ball that clipped the prolific batsman's top edge and was smartly taken by Jack Ikin at second slip. The England fielders raised their arms in triumph, but Bradman didn't flinch. Captain Wally Hammond then appealed to umpire George Borwick who, perhaps confused by Bradman's refusal to walk, ruled not out.

There was little doubt around the ground that Borwick had made a mistake. Even Keith Miller on the Australian dressing room balcony, who would've been the next man in, thought his teammate was out as he instinctively rose from his seat and grabbed his gloves and bat.

There was widespread disbelief among the England side and Hammond was livid. As he walked past Bradman at the end of the over, he said: 'A fine bloody way to start a series.'

It proved to be a turning point. Bradman returned after lunch to make a huge hundred before a thunderstorm transformed the uncovered wicket and Australia strolled to victory. A series win followed and Miller was sure that much hinged on that one moment: 'Not only the result of the match, but the result of the whole series of Tests, may have depended on that one decision.'

● LAMB TO THE SLAUGHTER

If it was good enough for Don Bradman, it was certainly good enough for England's (well, South Africa's) Allan Lamb in the opening Test of the 1982-83 Ashes at Perth. He refused to walk when Dennis Lillee induced a thick edge from the batsman. In Lamb's words: 'I stood there and hoped for the best. The greatest danger to the slips was being injured by one of the splinters.'

Amazingly, the umpire's finger was not raised and Lillee went berserk. 'I then got the most abuse I've ever heard, before or since,' said Lamb.

When he was eventually dismissed, Lamb was escorted back to the pavilion by wicketkeeper Rod Marsh, who informed the batsman: 'Just making sure you go this time and don't change your mind, you South African bastard!'

The silence of the Lambs (after publication of this picture).

● GOING BRIGHT RED

Another famous non-walker of that era was Geoffrey Boycott, who provoked a furious response from the Australians during the fourth Test at Headingley in 1977.

Spinner Ray Bright was convinced he'd managed to snare the great Yorkshireman with a faint edge as Boycott tried to turn him to leg, but the appeal was turned down and Bright saw red. He had to be physically restrained by captain Greg Chappell, such was his anger at the injustice.

Boycott's batting partner, Tony Greig, confirmed that he thought Bright was right to feel so aggrieved: 'Boycott was out without any shadow of a doubt. But why should he walk? None of the Aussies did.'

Boycott went on to reach his 100th first-class century, scoring 191 in all, as England won by an innings and 85 runs to secure the urn.

● TAKING A WHIPPING

Lord Harris's amateur England team that toured Australia in 1878-79 weren't playing for the Ashes – it was three years too early for that – but there was still plenty of ill feeling when they took on a New South Wales team in Sydney.

When local hero and future Australia captain Billy Murdoch was ruled run out by umpire George Coulthard when on 10, the crowd smelled a rat. Many of them had money staked on the match and they sensed foul play, as Coulthard was a Victorian who had been brought to stand in the Tests by Harris.

A pitch invasion followed the decision, in which the players were forced to defend themselves with stumps from the angry mob, one of whom managed to strike Lord Harris with a whip. One of Harris's teammates, Albert 'Monkey' Hornby, chased and caught the assailant as chaos reigned, but Harris stood his ground and refused to change the umpire or forfeit the match.

Instead, once the situation had calmed down, he wrote an angry letter to the authorities: 'We never expect to see scenes of such disorder again; we can never forget this one.' It was an embarrassment for New South Wales cricket, almost as embarrassing as the match, in which Lord Harris's team completed a victory – but only after a break for the Sabbath of course.

● BOYCOTT'S ER ... BOYCOTT

What is it about run outs and their wonderful ability to create controversy, altercations and the occasional full-scale riot? Sadly, in this age of the 'third umpire' we no longer trust the official's naked eye on the pitch, meaning a distinct dearth of run-out riots these days.

Having been bowled a cap and ball, Boycott didn't know which one to hit.

One mad moment of argy-bargy occurred during the fiery 1970-71 Ashes series when it seemed that a player only had to look at his opposite number's boots the wrong way and all hell would break loose.

At the centre of the storm was Geoff Boycott at his stubborn best – and, in case you've lived on another planet for the last fifty years, that is particularly stubborn. He took on a run against Ian Chappell at Adelaide and came out second best according to umpire Max O'Connell. But Boycs was having none of it and promptly hurled his bat down to the ground in disgust.

Within seconds, Boycott was surrounded by angry fielders, pointing towards the pavilion and manhandling him. Cricket this was not, to coin a phrase. When Boycott eventually returned to the pavilion, he was accompanied by a colossal wall of booing from the restless natives.

He had the last laugh, though, and the locals were soon applauding him when he returned to the crease for the second innings and made a typically defiant century.

● DECLARING FRUSTRATION

New rules generally cause confusion in most sports, and cricket, which has a fairly complex set of laws, is no exception. In the fourth Test at Old Trafford in 1921, England were attempting to reverse an eight-match losing streak when captain Lionel Tennyson tried to declare the England innings late on the second day.

The new rules prevented any declarations with less than 100 minutes to go on the first day of a Test and, as the first day of this match had been lost to the Manchester rain, Australia captain Warwick Armstrong believed day two was effectively day one.

Armstrong sat on the pitch in protest as the crowd heckled and booed but, after a 25-minute hiatus, the umpires agreed with him and the England innings continued, only for Armstrong to break the rules himself. He had bowled the last over before his 'sit-in' and he then bowled the first over once play restarted, meaning he'd illegally bowled consecutive overs. But, standing 6ft 2in and weighing in at 22-stone, unsurprisingly nobody took up that particular point with him.

MY FAVOURITE ASHES MOMENT

ENGLAND OFF-SPINNER PETER SUCH

In Australia's first innings of the 1993 Ashes series at Old Trafford, Peter Such took six for 67 as the tourists were dismissed for 289. He takes up the story:

'Old Trafford would have to be the best moment. I was making my debut, so I was obviously nervous and excited about the prospect. Your debut is the game that you'll always remember and I was just fortunate that it went well for me. We had a lot of rain in the build-up to the match and, as a consequence, the Old Trafford pitch was a bit damp to start with.

'We won the toss and bowled, Australia got off to a good start, but at the back end of the day we managed to claw it back. You always remember your first wicket. Mine was David Boon. He nicked it, Chris Lewis was at first slip and he juggled it two or three times – I was thinking: "Has he caught it? Hasn't he? Oh no, hang on a minute ... Yes, he has!" Those sorts of emotions go through your mind in the space of a split second.

'The real notable wickets for me as an off-spinner were, firstly, bowling Steve Waugh through the gate and hitting his off stump. From an off-spinning perspective, that's your ultimate dismissal: getting someone driving, going through the gate then hitting the top of off stump. It doesn't get much better than that. Then, on the second morning, I had Allan Border stumped. Given the stature of the bloke and the player that he was, I took a lot from it. When it all clicked on the second morning, I was thinking: "Blimey, I'm on fire here!"

'When England batted, Such's fellow Ashes debutant Shane Warne stole the headlines by dismissing Mike Gatting with what was to become known as "The ball of the century".

'It was one of those things. It didn't take the gloss off what I'd achieved, but it diverted attention away from what, for me, had been a fantastic first innings. I was sitting out on the balcony at the time. At Old Trafford back then, we were square-on so didn't know exactly what had happened. So I hopped inside to see the TV replay and I thought: "What the hell happened there?"'

Peter Such spontaneously levitated after taking his first Test wicket.

83

CHAPTER FIVE

THE TOP 10 AUSTRALIA ASHES HEROES

Runs and wickets are the usual criteria for cricket hero worship, but not in these parts. The legends included in this section also offered something extra. Some of them became cult heroes for a relatively minor but significant action, some were just hellraisers who were more likely to make the front pages than the back, while others were brave or had the right character and attitude for such an intense sporting contest. For those reasons, and more, these are the men who have helped shape Australia's Ashes history more than any others.

⚪ 1. WARWICK ARMSTRONG

Never mind the Ashes, there's a pretty strong case for Warwick Armstrong to be on a list of the Top 10 all-time Australian Heroes. One of the greatest captains in Australian cricket history – if not the greatest – this larger-than-life character won eight of his ten Ashes Tests as skipper and proved to be one of his country's finest ambassadors while touring England.

The England fans became intoxicated by Armstrong and his all-conquering 1921 team – it's hard to imagine Allan Border or Ricky Ponting enjoying such adulation while touring England in recent times – to the point that he would be serenaded by outbursts of 'For he's a jolly good fellow' when visiting theatres and would always be surrounded by fans in public.

Armstrong's twenty-year career saw him become bigger and bigger, both in terms of his success and his actual size. By the time he was captaining the Aussies in his early forties, he tipped the scales at 22 stone – he wasn't known as 'The Big Ship' for nothing. And, when he once took in an evening of boxing in England, the *Evening News* reported: 'He was attired in evening dress and really looked more formidable than any of the heavyweights.' He would certainly have given Freddie Flintoff a contest in the ring.

In the 1920-21 series, Armstrong's heroics included three centuries, the last of which was made while battling malaria with the aid of a couple of medicinal whiskies. The illness limited his bowling, but his will to win was such that he batted right through it as he led his side to a record 5-0 mauling of the Poms.

As if that wasn't enough, a couple of months later Armstrong was on a ship bound for England to defend the urn, but the skipper was unhappy with his bulk. While most of his teammates were relaxing on the long journey, Armstrong spent a few hours of each day shovelling coal in the ship's boiler house to improve his fitness. It paid off, too, as another series win followed.

Like all great Ashes heroes, Armstrong was also partial to a bit of gamesmanship. In the 1909 Oval Test, debutant England batsman Frank Woolley would have been a tad nervous as he walked to the wicket to face Armstrong. But the Australian had no intention of letting Woolley settle, as he bowled a series of trial balls while

Woolley waited. And waited. And waited some more. In fact, it was fully 18 minutes before play actually restarted.

Twelve years later, The Oval crowd were certainly more amused by Armstrong's antics during the last few overs of his final Test. With the hard work of retaining the urn all done, Armstrong had positioned himself in the outfield when a discarded newspaper flew by in the breeze. He nonchalantly picked it up and began reading while the match continued. After the game, when he was asked what he'd been reading, he replied: 'I wanted to see who we were playing.'

Warwick Armstrong always liked to bat with a child's cap on.

● 2. JEFF THOMSON

Let's get one thing out of the way – he didn't have a moustache. But he's no less of a hero because of that slight omission. 'Thommo' terrorised English batsmen. He tormented them, he terrified them and, quite often, he caused them considerable physical pain (just ask David Lloyd).

And when he was done with the Pommie batsmen, he turned his attention to the Pommie journalists, famously frightening one respected English cricket writer by asking him: 'Are you one of those Pommie bastards who've been writing all that sh*t about me?'

Seconds later, Thommo fell flat on his face

When he wasn't busily threatening to become the fastest, deadliest bowler of all time, he spent his time threatening violence on the pitch. Before the infamous 'Bouncer War' 1974-75 series began in Brisbane, he wrote in a newspaper that he enjoyed 'hitting a batsman more than getting him out. I like to see blood on the pitch.'

But with all that aggression, there was definitely a lighter side to Thommo. When he and Lillee's partnership was at its height, the pair appeared on Australian television together and were asked what they would you do if they discovered they only had 30 minutes to live.

'I'd make love to the first thing that moved!' replied Lillee.

'And what would you do, Jeff?' asked the TV interviewer.

'I wouldn't move for half an hour!' said Thomson.

On the 1975 Ashes tour, when the unlikely grey-haired, bespectacled England debutant David Steele arrived at the wicket for the first time at the age of 33, Thomson remarked: 'Who's this then, Father bloody Christmas?'

On another tour, Thomson couldn't resist the power of the Jaguar he'd been given to drive and was stopped by police doing 120mph on the motorway – fast on the pitch, even faster off it, but it was losing that truly brought out the worst in the Aussie.

When he and Allan Border had taken Australia to within four runs of the unlikeliest victory in the 1982 Boxing Day Test at Melbourne, history beckoned as the last-wicket pair would have also won the Ashes with the match. When all hope had seemed lost, the pair put on 70 and were standing on the brink of the most famous of all wins when Ian Botham induced an edge from the bowler which was dropped by Chris Tavaré but scooped up by Geoff Miller. Cue bedlam. Especially when a devastated Thomson visited the English dressing room to let rip about what lay ahead for them in Sydney – it was in stark contrast to the close finish at Edgbaston in 2005 when Flintoff embraced Brett Lee; none of that namby-pamby nonsense for our Thommo.

● 3. SHANE WARNE

On Friday 4 June 1993, Shane Warne changed the course of Ashes history forever. Here's how Jonathan Agnew described the moment on *Test Match Special*: 'Shane Warne's coming on and taking off his floppy hat to reveal a shock of blond hair. There's an earring in one ear as well. He's certainly a member of the new generation of international cricketers with a modern-style haircut. He hasn't got a ponytail, he's got one of these new shave jobs; a number two or three razor round the back and rather more hair on top.

'Anyway, here he comes on now, he's going to bowl from the far end from which Peter Such did all the damage in Australia's innings ... I just wonder if there must be pressure on young Warne's shoulders here, because he will know that his team are expecting him to come on and take some wickets here or at least turn the ball.

'He's rehearsing one or two deliveries to Brendon Julian ... and here comes Shane Warne. Off only two or three paces, he bowls and Gatting is taken on the pad ... he's bowled! Well, Gatting is still standing there and he can't believe it. Well, that must have turned a

Warne bowls a rare beamer.

very long way. Gatting can't believe it. That is Shane Warne's first delivery in a Test match in England and he's comprehensively bowled Mike Gatting... That, I'm sure, will send a shockwave right through the England dressing room.'

In that one moment in Manchester when he stunned Mike Gatting, Warne not only turned a ball more than anyone could ever remember seeing, he also potentially won the series for Australia and exerted a psychological hold on all England batsmen that was to last until 2007. And for that reason alone, he's an Aussie Ashes hero.

Yes, he may have taken a record 195 wickets in his 36 Ashes Tests and all that, but how effective would he have been without that one magic moment at Old Trafford? With so much of sport played out in the mind, here was a player who revelled in drilling right inside his opponents' heads and winning the battle before he'd even released the ball from his hand.

And with that ball, he implanted a lorry-load of doubt into the minds of a generation of England batsmen, which meant England couldn't even think about winning the Ashes for another 12 years. Even now, when Warne threatens to make a comeback for the next Ashes series, he instils a modicum of fear in every Englishman's heart, despite the fact he would most likely be highly ineffective. Stranger things have happened...

● 4. DENNIS LILLEE

'I try to hit a batsman in the rib cage when I bowl a purposeful bouncer, and I want it to hurt so much that the batsman does not want to face me any more.'

Do we need to go any further?

Think of the headband, the hair, the relatively modest but always bristling moustache; Dennis Lillee *was* Australia. He *was* the Ashes. He even managed to heroically survive a serious back injury, which many thought would end his career, to return after more than 18 months out and form a devastating partnership with Jeff Thomson. We've already heard about him greeting the Queen and Prince Philip with a 'G'day', but there's more. After the 1977 Centenary Test, the players were introduced to the Queen, and Lillee pulled out a pen and paper from his jacket and asked for her autograph. She politely declined, although Lillee was lucky enough to receive an official signed photo of that precise moment from Buckingham Palace instead.

Former England captain Mike Brearley sums up our case for Lillee's Ashes hero status perfectly, saying: 'Dennis had a vivid presence on the field' and going on to describe him as 'irritating' and 'even a bit delinquent'.

Luckily, the batsman decided to search for his contact lens at just the right moment.

● 5. DON BRADMAN

It's not for the 99 average in Test cricket. And it's not for the 89 average in Ashes Tests. It's also not for the mind-boggling eleven centuries, six double-centuries and two triple-centuries he racked up against the Poms. No, Bradman's inclusion in this list is purely because of his attitude.

It's no good just being the best batsman in the history of the game, you need the swagger to go with it. And the Don had that in spades. After he stunned England by making an unbeaten 309 in a single day at Headingley in 1930, still a record, the story goes that he told his teammates: 'That wasn't a bad bit of practice. I'll be able to have a go at them tomorrow.'

His will to win was almost as impressive as his ability. During a tour match, Jack Fingleton was fielding at short leg when he was struck by a devastating blow from an England batsman. The ball had been hit straight at Fingleton, clipping his head then climbing ten feet in the air. As Fingleton lay in a semi-conscious state on the pitch, Bradman was heard to call 'Catch it, catch it!'

Keith Miller recalled the first post-war Ashes Test at Brisbane in 1946-47, when a surreal air hung over the game as the cricketers tried to return to normality after the horrific previous seven years. But Bradman was unemotional when it came to the business of beating

The early spot the ball competitions were extremely tough.

England and instructed Miller to bowl faster at Wally Hammond and Bill Edrich and to 'grind them into the dust'.

Those foolish enough to try any 'mental disintegration' (sledging to you and me) on Bradman soon regretted it, as Essex wicketkeeper Frank Rist testified. In 1948, Rist was on the receiving end as the tourists smashed an incredible 721 in a day against the county side at Southend. In one over Bradman was facing, he sent the first three balls, which had pitched on the off stump, to the cover boundary for four. 'Can't you hit them anywhere else?' asked Rist. The next three balls were pitched in the same place, but Bradman pulled them through mid-wicket for another trio of boundaries. He turned to Rist at the end of the over and said simply: 'How's that?'

Best of all about Bradman was that he never lost that strut and self-belief, even as he aged. In his later years, when a reporter asked him what he thought he would average against today's bowlers, he replied: 'I think I might have averaged about 38 or 39 perhaps.'

'Do you mean you regard today's bowling as so much better?' gasped the surprised reporter.

'Oh no,' said the Don. 'What you asked was what do I think I would have averaged today, and the answer is 38 or 39. Don't forget that today I'm 84 years old!'

● 6. STEVE WAUGH

You want heroics? You really want heroism? How about batting on one leg, is that good enough for you? Well, that's not even the half of it. How about batting on one leg and making a century in a dead rubber, so you needn't even have put yourself through all that pain? There you go: that's proper heroism.

Steve Waugh is an Ashes legend, having played in nine series and ended up on the losing side only once. Yet, it's his performance at The Oval in 2001 that will long be remembered as that of the ultimate competitor.

Having captained the side to the verge of retaining the urn, Waugh tore his calf muscle and had to leave the field while his teammates duly wrapped up victory. The Aussies were 3-0 up with two Tests to play and Waugh's job was done. He could put that injured leg up and watch the remaining Tests. Except he had other ideas.

He spent the fourth Test recuperating and picked himself to play in the final match after England had had the temerity to win the Headingley game. At The Oval, he limped, hobbled and winced his way through run after run until one final scrambled single earned him a remarkable century. And then he made another 57 just in case anyone thought that was it. Once Australia had more than 600 on the board, he declared, stood in the slips to oversee England being dismissed twice and then, and only then, was it time to return to Australia.

● 7. FRED SPOFFORTH

Never mind the extraordinary spell of bowling at The Oval in 1882 which won Australia the Test match and created the Ashes, consider this story about 'The Demon' as told by Charles Thornton to *Wisden*: 'Spofforth was at his happiest in country matches where his stories – always told with an air of sincerity – used to amuse people immensely. I would say to him at lunch, "How did you learn to be such a fine short-slip, Spoff?" And he would reply, "When I was quite young, I made a boy, when out for a walk, throw stones into a hedge, and as the sparrows flew out I caught 'em."'

Australia's first lightning-fast bowler, Spofforth was a Merv Hughes-like character. A man of principle, he refused to take his place when selected to play against the MCC in the first Test match in 1877 because wicketkeeper Billy Murdoch was not in the team, and only when Murdoch was called up for the next game did he make his debut.

And, as we've seen elsewhere, Spofforth was not afraid to mix it, as his showdown with Grace at The Oval in 1882 clearly illustrates. Put simply, no Spofforth, no Ashes.

8. MERV HUGHES

There have been plenty more talented cricketers to play for Australia than Merv Hughes but, in truth, he makes this list exclusively for his almost unrivalled moustache – and for everything that utter beast on his upper lip says about his character. So much was the facial walrus part of the man and the mythology, that reports surfaced claiming Hughes had insured it for £225,000 during his career. But, when interviewed for this book, Hughes cleared up that myth once and for all: 'I read that story, it's a load of crap,' he said. 'My moustache has never been insured. There was a shonky marketing person in Australia that put that out. I'd done a bit of work with him and, suffice to say, I haven't worked with him since.'

Hughes experienced the highs and lows of Ashes cricket, having been part of the Australia team defeated at home by England in 1986-87, but also playing a role in their victories in 1989 and, most notably, in 1993 when he took 31 wickets in the series. Graeme Hick came under a constant barrage that summer from Hughes, who would deliver his stock lines like: 'Does your husband play cricket as well?' and 'Mate, if you turn the bat over you'll see the instructions on the back.' Just another day at the office for Merv. And his moustache.

9. ERNIE JONES

Think of the 'ball of the century' and you no doubt conjure up an image of Mike Gatting's bewildered chubby face after Shane Warne's incredible introduction to Ashes cricket at Old Trafford in 1993. That may well have been the ball of the 20th century, but Ernie Jones has every right to claim he bowled the ball of the 19th century in 1896.

The *Wisden Cricketers' Almanack* claims this took place in the traditional tour opener between the tourists and Lord Sheffield's XI at Sussex, although it is often attributed to the first Test at Lord's a few weeks later. Either way, the facts are not disputed (much).

Jones was bowling to W.G.Grace and, far from being intimidated by the legendary hirsute Englishman, the Aussie sprinted to the crease and unleashed a devilish delivery which reared up at Grace, is said to have passed straight through his not inconsiderable beard and continued to soar over the wicketkeeper for four byes.

'What do you think you're at, Jonah?' enquired a clearly rattled Grace.

'Sorry, Doctor, she slipped,' replied Jones, who went on to strike Grace in the chest and break the ribs of another English batsman, Stanley Jackson.

He took 64 Test wickets (all but four of them English) and while this would be good enough to make him an honorary Aussie hero, the real reason for his inclusion is his post-Test career as a searcher and watcher for the Department of Trade and Customs in Fremantle. From his post on the docks, whenever an England touring team would arrive for the Ashes he would row out to greet them, crying repeatedly 'You haven't got a chance!' Now, *that's* heroic.

● 10. DOUG WALTERS

Walters was the Phil Tufnell of Australian cricket, which makes him a rather unlikely choice for an Australia Ashes Heroes Top 10. The batsman was so laid-back he was almost horizontal and his happy-go-lucky attitude made him a fans' favourite. Like them, he appeared to be interested only in where the next fag, drink or bet was coming from.

He was never a great success when touring England, but he saved his heroics for the home Ashes series, most memorably in the 1974-75 Perth Test when he scored a century in a session, complete with a six from the last ball of the day, bowled by Bob Willis. When he returned to the dressing room to receive his deserved hero's welcome, he was stunned to find it deserted and began cursing his teammates under his breath. Suddenly, his captain Ian Chappell emerged from the showers and reprimanded him for taking on a risky shot from the last ball of the day, before suddenly breaking out into a grin, at which point the rest of the team appeared from the showers and the mother of all Walters-style parties began.

Even when he was dropped from the national team, he was able to look on the bright side, remarking: 'Beauty! I won't have to be up early for nets.' On another occasion when spinner Ashley Mallett was hit for three consecutive sixes, Walters joked: 'Well, that's the reds gone. Now you can start on the colours.'

'There will never be another like him,' Dennis Lillee once said. 'I never saw him throw a bat, never heard him talk badly of anyone. He was so cool. He could bat, too.'

But let's be honest. The real reason why he's in this Top 10 is purely because of his pioneering achievement of setting the first Australia to England Ashes flight drinking record of 44 cans of beer in 1977.

● 11. UNSUNG HERO: FRED TATE

Fred Tate was English. He played one Ashes Test match in his career and it was for England against Australia. So what's he doing here? Well, without dear old Fred's 'heroics', Australia would never have won the amazing 1902 Ashes series in England.

Tate was selected as a bowler for the crucial fourth Test at Old Trafford at the last minute and, as a result, he couldn't find a hotel and was forced to stay in someone's attic – a far cry from the five-star accommodation enjoyed by today's cotton-wool-wrapped stars.

The match was a nail-biting affair, with Australia holding a 37-run first-innings lead, but they were struggling on a damp pitch at 16 for three second time around. At this point, Joe Darling offered a chance to Tate at deep square leg, which he put down. Darling went on to top score with 37 in a stand worth 48 before the next wicket fell. *Wisden* noted at the time, 'Unquestionably this, the only stand of the innings, determined the issue of the tensely close struggle.'

Australia were bowled out for 86, leaving England 124 to win on a rapidly deteriorating wicket – and they almost got there. At 116 for nine, that man Tate came to the wicket with fate and history weighing hard on his inexperienced shoulders. When he edged the first delivery he faced for four, the miracle seemed possible. However, he was clean bowled with the next ball to not only hand Australia victory by three runs but also give them the urn, and complete his personal nightmare as a Test debutant. It was his first and last international and Aussie cricket fans should still celebrate his 'achievement' to this very day.

MY FAVOURITE ASHES MOMENT

AUSTRALIA PACE BOWLER
BRETT LEE

'The second Test at Edgbaston in 2005 is the game that I've spoken most about during my playing career and for many reasons. We all know the outcome of that Test, but it was the way in which it was played.

'As soon as the game was over, Freddie Flintoff came up to me, put his arm around me and said something like: "Awesome game, bad luck, I thoroughly enjoyed the game." The photo of the two of us has become famous and represents the true spirit of cricket. I loved the way Freddie played the game, he played as hard as anyone, but afterwards he was ready to shake your hand and have a chat and a beer. It was true sportsmanship.

'That moment was very special for me and cemented a great bond between us. Our relationship off the field was formed because of how hard we played on the field. We played for different teams but belonged to the same club. Rest assured I still wanted to beat him every time I came up against him, and I know he thought the same way.'

Brett Lee celebrates the only known case of a batsman being bowled before the ball had reached the stumps.

CHAPTER SIX

THE TOP 10 ENGLAND ASHES HEROES

You know the drill by now – these are the players who have done the most to help shape England's Ashes history. They may not all appear at the top of the averages, but they will certainly have cropped up at the head of every pub or bar cricket conversation, due to making an impact that went beyond the game. We salute you, noble Englishmen, well Engl-ish-men as, like all the best England cricket line-ups, some of these players aren't actually English at all.

● 1. IAN BOTHAM

When you have an entire Ashes series named after you, it's fair to say you must have done something pretty heroic. The English summer of 1981 will forever be linked with Botham, thanks to his well-documented performances with ball and bat. But it's 'Beefy's' character on and off the pitch that really made him a hero to millions – and still does.

Like all the greatest sportsmen, Botham could be stubborn and single-minded, but he enjoyed life and was never afraid to get stuck in to any post-match activities. His high jinks include smoking cannabis, and assaulting a passenger on a flight while playing for Queensland – as Botham tells it, the arresting officer asked him to sign a bat before cautioning him.

During the 1980s, Botham was rarely off the front and back pages thanks to his extra-curricular activities (*see* Close of Play) and also because of quotes like this about his wife: 'I don't ask Kathy to face Michael Holding. So I don't see why I should be changing nappies.'

But, best of all, is his long-running feud with his Aussie nemesis Ian Chappell, which began in 1977 during the Centenary Test – a match in which Botham was not even playing. The two men remember what happened in very different ways – and we're certainly not going to take sides on this one. Beefy was playing club cricket in Australia at the time and, as he recalls, ran into Chappell in a bar and took exception to the Australian's Pommie-bashing, so he punched him and a full-scale brawl broke out which continued in the car park. Chappell's version of events is somewhat different, claiming that Botham pushed him off his chair, before he left the pub refusing to fight because: 'You either finish up in jail or hospital and I don't intend visiting either over a c*nt like you.'

Either way, the animosity between the pair has never ended and it all kicked off again during the 2010-11 Ashes when they clashed outside the Adelaide Oval after the fourth day's play. Botham was waiting for a car to pick him up as Chappell walked past and muttered something provocative. Before long, the pair were at each other's throats and had to be separated. An Australian Channel 9 source told the *Daily Mail*: 'They went for each other all right and it could have got very nasty if there hadn't been people on hand to keep them apart. They reacted quickly because we all know the history between these two. They might be aged 55 and 67, but neither of them are the type of people to give an inch in the face of conflict.'

We await the next instalment with baited breath.

● 2. ANDREW FLINTOFF

We all know the story but that doesn't make it any less impressive. After playing an instrumental role in helping England win back the Ashes for the first time in almost 19 years, Freddie decided to have himself a few drinks. In fact, he decided to have almost 19 years' worth of drinks in a fitting tribute to England's glorious summer of 2005.

The problem for Freddie was that he forgot to go to sleep and was still drinking the morning after when an open-top bus parade and a visit to meet the prime minister at 10 Downing Street had been arranged.

His escapades that famous morning included being unable to walk out of a building in a straight line, giving drunken television interviews in Trafalgar Square, having the word 'Twat' written on his forehead by best mate Steve Harmison and, allegedly, urinating in Tony Blair's garden. Whether he really peed on the prime minister's geraniums is neither here nor there, because on that day, Flintoff cemented his lifetime hero status.

He repeated the heroics in 2009, but with a lot less alcohol. By this time, injuries had taken their toll on his large frame. The England selectors did their best to nurse him through it all, and he bowled through the pain to help inspire England to victory, most notably at Lord's. 'I knew if I stopped I wouldn't start again,' he says. 'I finished Cardiff in bits, I'd had injections in my knees, I was taking all the painkillers. It got to the point where I was getting up to go to the Test match and was having problems dressing myself – Rachael [Flintoff's wife] was helping me – I'd get to the ground, have my jab, have my painkillers and I was all right, I'd get on with it. I wasn't thinking long-term, I knew it was my last four Test matches and I was just thinking about getting through them.' Stirring stuff.

He'll also always be remembered for his sporting act in consoling Brett Lee after England's amazing two-run win at Edgbaston in 2005, but let's gloss over that for this isn't the time or place for sentimentality and slushiness.

It was an ill-advised moment for the batsman to inspect the pitch.

3. FRANK TYSON

Tyson is no England hero. In fact, he's a bona fide England superhero, the only one of his kind on this list. For how else do you explain the following true story?

On the 1954-55 tour of Australia, England had been humbled in the first Test at Brisbane and were on the receiving end again in their first innings at Sydney. England bowler Tyson, in particular, had been in the wars when he turned his back on a Ray Lindwall bouncer and was cracked on the head so hard that he immediately collapsed to the ground, out cold – these were the days before helmets.

He was more or less dragged back to the dressing room and lay on the massage table as doctors and teammates tried to bring him out of his semi-conscious stupor.

Captain Len Hutton wrote in his autobiography: 'When he came out of his concussed state, I swear there was a new light in his eyes as if a spark had been kindled deep down inside him. I am not given to fanciful imagination, and the fact is that when he resumed bowling the next day he was a yard, maybe a yard and a half quicker than before. His pace on that decisive and extraordinary day in Sydney was nothing short of frightening.'

Marvel Comics themselves couldn't have come up with a better story, and it just got better and better for Tyson and England. So frightening was his pace that his own slip cordon all had to move back as he tore through the Aussies twice to claim ten wickets in the match and lead England to victory.

In the next Test at Melbourne he took nine wickets, followed by six at Adelaide as England wrapped up the series. What's more, Tyson even began to speak like a man possessed: 'To bowl quick is to revel in the glad animal action; to thrill in physical prowess and to enjoy a certain sneaking feeling of superiority over the other mortals who play the game. No batsman likes quick bowling and this knowledge gives one a sense of omnipotence.'

In all, he took 28 wickets in that Ashes win – and it was all thanks to Ray Lindwall. What's that they say about truth being stranger than fiction?

● 4. TONY GREIG

If there was one winner in the Bouncer War series of 1974-75 (other than Australia) it was the late, great (South African-born) England all-rounder Tony Greig. With Lillee and Thomson in full flight and causing England's batsmen a lethal combination of mental and physical pain, Greig's one-man stand against the first-Test battering of Brisbane was an act of extreme bravery.

Greig arrived at the crease with England 57 for four and had seen enough teammates lose their wickets, including two who had suffered broken bones in their hands after succumbing to the Aussies' intimidation. 'I decided to attack them, otherwise we were going to be fodder,' said Greig. 'I also decided to try and stir them up a little bit.'

He certainly did that. Not only did he take on the fearsome Australian quickies, he goaded them every time he struck a boundary by signalling the four like an umpire himself. As Ian Chappell, Australia's captain at the time, recalled, Lillee was livid: 'That obviously antagonised Dennis enormously. There weren't too many people around in world cricket at that stage who were looking to antagonise Dennis, but Tony did it, and he carried it off by scoring 110.'

Greig's behaviour might have earned the grudging respect of his opposite number, but his own teammates were somewhat less impressed with his antics. After Greig had signalled another four, one of his batting partners, tailender Derek Underwood, was heard to plead from the non-striker's end: 'Please don't make him mad.'

Unfortunately, Greig's heroics were not enough to save England, in either the Test or the series, but they were more than enough to earn him a place in this line-up.

● 5. EDDIE PAYNTER

Amid the drama and deceit of the infamous Bodyline series in 1932-33, one man rose above it all to become a hero to both the English and Australians.

On the second day of the decisive fourth Test at Brisbane, Eddie Paynter was taken seriously ill in the blistering heat and admitted to hospital with a high fever and acute tonsillitis. Australia had scored 340 and, as England batted on the third day, Paynter listened to proceedings in Brisbane General with injured teammate Bill Voce. As wickets fell steadily throughout the day, with England struggling, Paynter had heard enough. After instructing Voce to order a taxi, he put on his dressing gown and, ignoring the desperate calls of the nurses, made his way to The Gabba.

To the shock of captain Douglas Jardine and his England teammates, Paynter appeared in the dressing room and calmly put on his cricket whites and pads and made his way out to the middle at the fall of the next wicket, with England 216 for six. Incredibly, despite being barely able to move and also refusing Aussie captain Bill Woodfull's generous offer of a runner, Paynter managed to hang on until the close of play unbeaten on 24, as England moved on to 271 for eight.

After a standing ovation from the Australian spectators (which was quite something for an Englishman at the best of times, let alone during the Bodyline series), Paynter returned to hospital overnight, but – armed with medicine and tablets – was back at The Gabba the following morning to continue his innings.

After two breaks to gargle with medicine, Paynter was eventually out for 83 and England had a first-innings lead of 16. He even insisted on fielding during the first part of Australia's second innings, but was soon back in hospital again to listen to the Aussies wilting to just 175 all out.

He made one final triumphant return to The Gabba from hospital as England chased 160 to clinch the Ashes and, in a fairytale ending, it was Paynter who was at the crease to hit Stan McCabe for six as England regained the urn.

Honourable mention should also be made of Denis Compton's heroics at Old Trafford in 1948 when he top-edged a Ray Lindwall bouncer into his forehead. Several stitches and brandies later, Compton strode back to the wicket and made an unbeaten 145, which caused BBC TV commentator Leslie Mitchell to say: 'Great as Compton is, never has he been greater.' But not great enough for an exclusive slot in this line-up.

● 6. PHIL TUFNELL

If Doug Walters is in the Top 10 Australia Ashes Heroes, Tuffers is certainly making it on to England's list. If a case for his inclusion was really needed, it's hard to look further than the answer Tufnell gave when asked why he opted to become a spin bowler: 'You cannot smoke twenty a day and bowl fast.'

From the moment he was called into England's squad for the 1990-91 Ashes tour, it was quite clear Tuffers was going to liven up proceedings for fans – the Australian crowds took to him, perhaps due to his utterly inept fielding and rabbit-in-headlights batting. Most famously, one wag once called to him, 'Hey Tuffers! Can you lend me your brain? I'm building an idiot.'

He was always one to see the funny side of events, as Mike Atherton noted in his autobiography, Tufnell was particularly perturbed at Shane Warne's arrival on the scene, complaining: 'That bloke's making me look ordinary! He's ruining my career!'

Other memorable moments, like going on the run from psychiatrists in Perth and falling out with Aussie umpires, have already been mentioned in these pages to show that, when it comes to England's most disastrous post-war Ashes era, Tuffers was the man who often provided rare rays of sunshine in between the stormy clouds of sound beatings at the hands of Australia.

● 7. HAROLD LARWOOD

He may well have been the monkey to Douglas Jardine's organ grinder, but that doesn't mean Larwood's Bodyline batterings are any less deserving of recognition. Such was the stranglehold that Larwood had over Australia's batsmen, even his mere presence on the field caused the opposition trouble. Even when the Ashes had already been won, and Larwood had broken a bone in his foot in the final Test, he stayed on the pitch at Jardine's insistence while Bradman was batting – just so that the great Australian wouldn't be allowed to settle and think that Larwood could no longer bowl.

Larwood explained his bowling philosophy in 1972: 'I used to give every new batsman four balls. One was a bouncer to check his courage, the second a fizzer to check his eyesight, the third was a slow one to try out his reflexes, and the fourth a bender to see if he was a good cricketer. If he took a single off each of the four balls, I knew I was in trouble.'

Underneath the hostility of Larwood's Bodyline bowling lay a gentle character who became an unlikely Australian when he emigrated in 1950 and befriended many of the Aussies whom he'd spent so long tormenting. Forgive and forget, how very English.

Having left his jacket at home, Larwood was forced to borrow one from Giant Haystacks.

8. DOUGLAS JARDINE

And so to the Bodyline organ grinder himself, the man who supposedly brought more shame on English cricket than the ECB chiefs when they jumped into bed with Allen Stanford. On the surface, there doesn't seem much heroic about devising a tactic which would deliberately cause opponents harm. But look at the context.

Don Bradman had come to England in 1930 and slayed every bowler who dared to chuck the red leather at him, notching an almost impossible 974 runs in the Test series. Jardine's Bodyline was simply a reaction to Bradman's brilliance; a cunning plan devised by watching footage of the master batsman and working out his weakness. 'I've got it, he's yellow!' was Jardine's famous Eureka moment. Unfortunately for Bradman's teammates, they would have to suffer with him.

But when your starting point was 'All Australians are uneducated and an unruly mob', as was Jardine's, Bodyline doesn't seem to be a particularly bad idea after all.

So unpopular was Jardine in Australia, it seems impossible not to include him in this list. When he arrived for the start of the tour, journalists requested he give them his England teams early on the day before the match as the papers went to press at noon. His dismissive reply was: 'Do you think we've come all this way to provide scoops for your bloody newspaper?'

Despite his tactics, Jardine – born in India to Scottish parents, which may explain Bodyline better than anything else – was no coward, as he showed when he took a fearful battering from a Queensland bowler in a tour match which followed the notoriously bad-tempered Adelaide Test. The England captain batted for more than an hour until the close of play despite being savagely struck on the hip bone, and when he returned to the dressing room he ordered the door to be shut before fainting on the massage table.

Occasionally, just occasionally, his steely on-pitch veneer peeled away to reveal his human side. When Bill Bowes dismissed Bradman with the first ball that he faced in the second Test, Jardine could not contain his excitement. Bowes wrote in his autobiography: 'Jardine, the sphinx, had momentarily forgotten himself for the one and only time in his cricketing life. In his sheer delight at this unexpected stroke of luck he had clasped both his hands above his head and was jigging around like an Indian doing a war dance.'

9. DAVID STEELE

He may have played only three Ashes Tests, but what an impact he made. Prior to 31 July 1975, you could have suggested any odds you liked on David Steele winning BBC Sports Personality of the Year and any rational bookmaker would have gladly taken your money while laughing maniacally in your face. Yet, within a month, the 33-year-old county cricket pro, who thought his moment had long gone, was a virtual shoe-in for the award.

When Tony Greig took over the England captaincy for the second Test, he asked county colleagues who was the toughest player to get out – the answer from almost everyone was David Steele. Not only did the spectacled, grey-haired Steele frustrate rampaging Aussies Dennis Lillee and Jeff Thomson, but he did it in the most English of ways, with the minimum of fuss. In his six Ashes innings he scored 50, 45, 73, 92, 39 and 66 as he took the battle to the Aussies. Such was his demeanour and style, the *Sun*'s Clive Roberts described him as 'The bank clerk who went to war' – only he almost missed his first engagement at Lord's.

'I had played at Lord's for twelve years, but always changed in the away dressing room,' he explained. 'We used the Middlesex one for England matches, but when I went out to bat I got confused, took one staircase too many and ended up going out the back door of the pavilion. I was a bit late getting to the wicket.'

Thomson famously compared him to 'Father bloody Christmas' while wicketkeeper Rod Marsh had plenty to say, although Steele was up to the sledging challenge, telling Marsh: 'Take a good look at this arse of mine, you'll see plenty of it this summer.' Not only was he right, but the Australians surprisingly backed down: 'After my first Test, the press asked Ian Chappell if they had sledged me much,'

110

said Steele. 'He said they didn't bother after a while because they realised I was in my own world.'

England had lost the only Test of the series in which Steele hadn't featured before he then helped them to three draws. The Ashes may have been lost, but the bank clerk certainly won the war.

The bank clerk struck a boundary before quickly cashing a cheque.

● 10. GARY PRATT

It's hard to believe that a player who has never been capped for England could join a list of such illustrious names as this, but without substitute fielder Gary Pratt, England might never have won the 2005 Ashes.

Consider this. The series is tied at 1-1, Australia are following on but starting to look like they might be back in the game at 155 for two, still 100 runs behind England, with captain Ricky Ponting well set on 48. Imagine Ponting staying at the wicket, making a big century – just as he did in the previous Test at Old Trafford to save

Australia – and the Aussies manage to get out of a hole. The series stays level, there's another draw at The Oval and Australia retain the Ashes, although England restore pride.

Without Pratt, that might well have been the outcome and the cricket world would be a very different place today for England and Australia fans.

As it happens, Damien Martyn took on a risky single to Pratt at cover point, whose perfect pick-up and throw caught Ponting a good yard out of his ground. The Australia captain then threw all his toys out of the pram, gesticulating and swearing towards the England dressing room, where he thought coach Duncan Fletcher was watching (in fact, as revealed by Pratt elsewhere in these pages, he wasn't), about his use of substitutes throughout the series. Australia battled on, but England eventually prevailed to take a 2-1 lead, which they clung on to at The Oval. The *Daily Telegraph* referred to Pratt's run out as 'one of the defining moments in Ashes history'.

It wasn't the first time England had benefited from a sub in the Ashes either. Back in 1930, the opening Test at Trent Bridge was building to a tremendous finish with Australia 229 for three, chasing 429 to win, and Don Bradman and Stan McCabe in full flow. Step forward, Sydney Copley. The substitute fielder, on for the sick Harold Larwood, took a wonderful full-length diving catch to dismiss McCabe and England eventually won by 93 runs.

Unfortunately for Copley and England, Australia dominated the rest of the series to win the urn and that's exactly why Pratt makes the Top 10 and Copley does not.

● 11. UNSUNG HERO: ERIC HOLLIES

He may have played only one Ashes Test, but Hollies deserves way more recognition for his achievement in the 1948 fifth Test at The Oval.

That's because this match was all about Don Bradman. The Aussies had strolled to another Ashes series win and this was Bradman's final Test where he needed only four runs in his final innings to guarantee himself a scarcely believable career Test average of 100.

As he came out on to the field, Bradman received a standing ovation from the English crowd and 'Three Cheers' from the England team as he arrived in the middle. Waiting to bowl to him was Hollies, on his Ashes debut. The situation couldn't have been better set up for the Don as all of Australia, and the cricket-playing world tuned in.

Bradman played defensively to the first ball, which was a leg break. The second delivery was a googly. The greatest batsman in the world pushed forward at the ball, missed it and was bowled through the gate for a duck. This is how commentator John Arlott described it on the radio: 'Two slips, a silly mid-off and a forward short-leg close to him, as Hollies pitches the ball up slowly and – he's bowled! [Forty seconds of complete silence as Bradman is applauded off the field] Bradman bowled Hollies, nought. Bowled Hollies, nought. And what do you say under those circumstances? How ... I wonder if you can see a ball very clearly in your last Test in England at a ground where you've played out some of the biggest cricket of your life and where the opposing team have just stood round you and given you three cheers and the crowd has clapped you all the way to the wicket. I wonder if you really see the ball at all.'

There went the 100 average, and there went decades' worth of crowing from Australia fans about Bradman's average, which would forever stand at a paltry 99.94. England cricket fans should really take this opportunity to thank the one and only Eric Hollies.

MY FAVOURITE ASHES MOMENT

ENGLAND BOWLER DEAN HEADLEY

The England paceman, who currently teaches cricket at Stamford School, once took six for 60 in a memorable England victory at Melbourne in 1998-99.

'I was involved in the longest Test session ever at Melbourne in 1998 – that was a very emotional session of high-intensity cricket and I did all right. One of the images that sticks in my mind is Darren Gough's war cry at the end of the match when he took McGrath's wicket with an inswinging yorker that trapped him LBW. He was waving a stump with his hand and shouted an expletive at the top of his voice, I couldn't tell exactly what it was, but it was "something off!" – it was a proper war cry!

'Goughie and I played only five Tests together, but we got 53 wickets between us, which is not bad. He had the same attitude as myself: if things don't go your way, you just keep going. And that's what we did in that game at Melbourne.

'The next Test at Sydney was the only match where we properly competed with Australia – in Melbourne, although we won, we had less of the possession of the game. We got to Sydney, and we went hammer and tongs with the Aussies. My only disappointment was that we had them on the run in the second innings, and Slater was given not out on 35, which was the biggest travesty really, because I ran him out with a direct hit and he was miles out [the decision was referred to the third umpire, but there were no clear camera angles], but went on to make 123. Michael Vaughan said recently if that 1998-99 side had come back from Australia with a 2-2 draw that would have been as big a result as winning the Ashes in 2005.

'Another great memory from a personal point of view was when I made my debut at Old Trafford in 1997. I hit Mark Taylor on the head very early on and ended up with eight wickets, which was a good result for me. It was interesting because I got three left-handers out in the first and second innings and all of a sudden I was called one of the best bowlers to left-handers in the world. I was coming back from injury in that Test and when I'm not on song I nip the ball back away from left-handers and it obviously helped that Australia had three of them. What was probably a deficiency if they'd had a side full of right-handers actually turned into an advantage. And then you get labelled for the rest of your life – you're the one that can bowl to left-handers!

'I remember being called George [Headley's cricket-playing grandfather's name] for the whole of my first Test match by Australia – but I think Australians only pick on people they think they can affect, so they give you a little nudge in a Test early on and if you don't take a blind bit of notice they don't target you with it.'

Headley had just heard that it was roast duck for lunch.

CHAPTER SEVEN

THE TOP 10 ASHES SERIES

What makes a brilliant Ashes series? The ingredients are many: tense games, extraordinary finishes, outstanding individual efforts, two evenly matched sides, a whole load of bad blood, awful umpiring decisions and a healthy measure of controversy. This chapter looks back at those series that had some, if not all, of those components, which means that players and spectators alike still talk about them to this very day. And now you can too.

● 1. BODYLINE – 1932-33

The yardstick by which all other Ashes series are measured, England's 1932-33 tour of Australia is quite simply the most controversial, talked-about and intense Test series in cricket history. It's hard to underestimate the shockwaves that were caused by Douglas Jardine's overly aggressive tactics in which predominantly leg-side fields were set and bowlers instructed to aim short-pitched deliveries at the batsmen – the rifts caused were felt as far away as Whitehall, where there were serious concerns that Bodyline might cause a deterioration in Anglo-Australian relations; a colonial catastrophe was not far off.

But were it not for the prolific form of Don Bradman, there would never have been Bodyline, or 'leg theory' as England skipper Jardine called it, as he decided this was the way to combat the great Australian. And it worked – Bradman's average was cut to a rather ordinary (by his standards) 56 for the series.

Jardine's plan relied on Harold Larwood and Bill Voce's bowling and the latter was not afraid to put the theory into practice.

England fans celebrate the Bodyline series win at a time when celebrating just meant standing around.

Before the series started he told Australia's Victor Richardson: 'If we don't beat you, we'll knock your bloody heads off!'

Despite the physical ambush, Australia managed to recover from the shock of losing the first Test (which Bradman missed through illness) to level the series in the second, but it was at Adelaide in the third Test where the contest reached its nadir. *Wisden* described it as 'the most unpleasant Test ever played', and Australia batsmen Bill Woodfull and Bert Oldfield would have doubtless agreed. Both men suffered badly although, ironically, their injuries occurred when Larwood was bowling to a conventional field and pitching the ball outside off stump. Woodfull was struck painfully above the heart while Oldfield fractured his skull, taking a blow that, an inch lower, might have killed him.

The Australian crowd booed and hissed almost every ball, and police had to position themselves between the spectators and the field of play as the threat of a full-scale riot became a serious possibility. Former England captain and tour manager Pelham Warner went to see Woodfull, who made his famous declaration: 'I don't want to see you, Mr Warner. There are two teams out there. One is playing cricket. The other is making no attempt to do so.'

After the match, the Australian board sent a message to the MCC asking for the Bodyline policy to be halted, claiming it to be 'unsportsmanlike'. This provoked outrage in England and there was talk of trade relations between the countries being damaged. England refused to play the final two Tests unless the 'unsportsmanlike' accusation was withdrawn. The Australians, sensing the damaging lasting economic effects of the cancellation of the tour, had no choice but to withdraw the accusation and the tour went on, with England claiming a 4-1 thrashing – it was their only Ashes victory between 1930 and 1953.

In terms of brutality and naked win-at-all-costs rivalry, this was the series that set the standard for all future Ashes contests. What's more, every Australian who pulls on a baggy green cap and every Englishman who wears the three lions goes into battle with that historical burden weighing heavy – in effect, the aftermath of Bodyline is still being played out every time the two countries collide. And that can only be a good thing.

● 2. BOTHAM'S ASHES – 1981

So much has been written. So many tapes have been replayed ad infinitum. Everyone knows the stories. But that doesn't mean that they're not worth hearing again, does it? This was, quite simply, an amazing Test series, which featured two of the most extraordinary matches ever played.

The summer had started badly for England and captain Ian Botham, who was still without a win under his stewardship after ten matches. Australia won an exciting low-scoring opener at Trent Bridge to leave Botham on the verge of quitting as captain going into the Lord's Test. And after bagging a pair in a stalemate, Beefy had had enough and offered his resignation, although chairman of selectors Alec Bedser confirmed the captain would have been relieved of his duties anyway.

With Botham out of form and England having appointed Mike Brearley as captain for the remainder of the series, there was serious talk of the all-rounder missing the next game at Headingley. Former captain Ray Illingworth had even written in his *Sunday Mirror* column that Botham was 'overweight, over-rated and overpaid'. (Despite such comments, this did not prevent Illingworth from leading English cricket in the following decade.)

Brearley, ever the master of psychology (literally, as he became a psychoanalyst in his post-cricket life), chatted with Botham before the Leeds match. The all-rounder recalled in his autobiography something of how their conversation went: 'Beef,' Brearley said. 'Are you sure you want to play? If you don't, I will fully understand.'

'Of course I bloody want to play, Brears,' replied Botham. 'I feel good about this match.'

'That's great. I think you'll get 150 runs and take ten wickets,' said Brearley, who was almost exactly right.

Unfortunately, the game didn't quite go according to plan for England, as Australia managed to score 401 for nine declared on a tough pitch, although Botham did claim six of those ten wickets Brearley had predicted. When England batted, Botham performed well with a rapid 50, but it was nowhere near enough to save his side, who were dismissed for 174 and, batting again, soon lost opener Graham Gooch for a duck before stumps on the Saturday ahead of the rest day.

Botham wrote that 'defeat was a foregone conclusion as far as everyone was concerned. So when both teams turned up at my house on the Saturday night for the traditional Botham barbecue, the mood in the camps could not have been more different. The party helped improve our mood, however, and we ended up in a rugby scrum on the lawn before the Aussies headed off back to their hotel around midnight.'

Could that scrum have changed the outcome of the match? It didn't seem likely as England succumbed to 135 for seven when play resumed on the Monday. Earlier that morning, the England players had checked out of their hotel, fearing the worst. Even Brearley had showered, changed and packed away his kit, although he kept a cricket shirt on in case he was picked out by TV cameras. But the game was over – England needed to score 92 more just to make Australia bat again. Trying to explain what happened next still leaves Botham struggling. He wrote: 'The truth is that it was just one of those crazy, glorious one-off flukes.'

Even with his bat raised high, the Aussies still couldn't claim Botham's wicket.

Graham Dilley joined Botham in the middle and the bowler began throwing his bat, which inspired Beefy to do the same. The rest is, of course, history as Botham smashed his way to an unbeaten 149, aided and abetted by Dilley's 56, then Chris Old's 29. Even Bob Willis hung around for long enough to stretch the lead to 129.

Which brings us to another curiosity in this utterly unbelievable match – Willis was not even meant to be playing. He'd been injured and ill, so the selectors had actually sent a letter to Mike Hendrick inviting him to play instead. When Bedser called Willis to tell him the bad news, the Warwickshire bowler was stunned and had to explain to the selector that he was fully fit and had missed his county's last match only to rest up for the Headingley Test [in those days such a concept was seemingly beyond the selectors' comprehension]. He offered to prove his fitness by playing a second XI game for his county, which he came through unscathed. Bedser then had to take the unusual step of asking the Derbyshire staff to intercept Hendrick's letter, which would have arrived the following morning – they duly sorted through the mail, found his invite and made sure he never received it.

And that's why, with Australia chasing 130 for victory, Willis was present to perform heroics and take eight for 43 to hand England the most unlikely victory of all which squared the series. Botham described Willis's effort as 'the most magnificent spell of sustained hostile bowling it has ever been my privilege to witness'.

The country had ground to a halt as England neared victory – people gathered around television shop windows on high streets, even trading at the Stock Exchange momentarily ceased. This was England's – and Botham's – summer; fate seemed to have decreed that, as was shown in another extraordinary climax to the fourth Test at Edgbaston.

A low-scoring match saw Australia chasing 151 for victory on a Sunday afternoon in Birmingham (this series was the first time Sunday cricket had been played in England). They were coasting at 105 for four when John Emburey managed to snag the key wicket of Allan Border for 40. Brearley tossed the ball to Botham, and 28 Beefy deliveries later the match was over. The all-rounder took five wickets for one run in a mesmerising spell, as the tourists fell apart for the second successive match.

Once again, he was modest about his achievement, writing: 'Sure, I had bowled fast and mainly straight – but enough to deserve those figures? Surely not. The Aussies had lost their bottle; there was no other explanation for it. In fact, I can recall the look on the faces of the Aussie batsmen as I ran in. It was exactly the same shell-shocked expression as I had seen at Headingley a fortnight earlier.'

England were now 2-1 up with two matches to play and, at Old Trafford in the fifth Test, the match was in the balance with the hosts 104 for five in their second innings, a lead of 205. Botham arrived at the wicket and hit a superb 118, which caused John Woodcock of *The Times* to write: 'Was this the greatest Test innings ever?' Whether it was or not, it inspired England to a 505-run lead which was too much for the tourists, who made a fight of it, but were bowled out for 402, meaning England had won the urn in a way no other side before them had ever done. And surely never will.

● 3. ENGLAND STOP THE ROT – 2005

First Test, Lord's, 21 July 2005 – Australia's captain, Ricky Ponting, has blood pouring from his cheek after being struck a vicious blow by Steve Harmison. Not a single England player bothers to check if he needs help. Ponting looks dazed and confused. And so the scene is set for possibly the most keenly contested Ashes series of them all, where no quarter was asked and none given. Everything was on the line as arguably the greatest Test side of all time, nearing the end of its reign, took on an England team, and a nation, that hadn't experienced Ashes success for a generation.

Harmison's opening salvo was impressive as he and the other England bowlers tore into Australia, who had won the toss and found themselves 190 all out before tea. But natural order was soon restored when England batted as Glenn McGrath's 500th Test wicket and four more for good measure gave the tourists a small first-innings lead, which they then extended to more than 400 in their second innings – it was too much for England, who were bundled out by McGrath and Shane Warne. First blood to Australia (literally), but England had showed enough to suggest the series might not be as one-sided as many feared. Not that the British press were bothered by that – they laid into England, with spinner Ashley Giles coming in for plenty of criticism.

And so to Edgbaston where two extraordinary moments occurred before a ball had been bowled, thus setting the tone for an astonishingly tense and nerve-shredding match. First, McGrath trod on a cricket ball and damaged his ankle ligaments in the warm-up, ruling him out of the match, then Ponting inexplicably chose to bowl after winning the toss. 'We fully expected him to bat,' said England skipper Michael Vaughan. 'Edgbaston generally deteriorates over a few days and spin comes into play.'

England capitalised on Ponting's gaffe by racking up 407 on the first day at a very Australia-esque scoring rate, and they managed to take a crucial 99-run first-innings lead, with Giles claiming three wickets including key batsmen Ponting and Michael Clarke. England struggled second time around, slumping to 101 for seven, but a crucial 73 from Andrew Flintoff (his second fifty of the game) steered them to 182, meaning Australia would need 282 to win.

They had made a promising start, with 47 on the board, but then Flintoff came on to bowl the over of his life, first clean bowling Justin Langer, then twice rapping Ponting on the pads before having him caught behind. 'It's probably the best over I've ever bowled,' he said. 'I was still on a high from my batting.'

Wickets continued to fall at a steady rate, with Australia closing day three on 175 for eight, miles away from winning and England potentially two balls from levelling the series, with Warne and Brett Lee at the crease. Despite the possibility of the match being over in minutes, a full house was waiting for the players the following morning, as a success-starved English public were desperate to see their team win a meaningful Ashes Test. It was a morning none of them would ever forget.

Warne and Lee added 45 to the overnight total before that man Flintoff bowled the spinner, or at least helped him to hit his own wicket. That brought McGrath's replacement Michael Kasprowicz to the crease with 62 still required for victory. Slowly but surely, the last-wicket pair picked their shots as they edged closer and closer to a hugely unlikely victory. Unbearable tension filled the Birmingham ground as the tourists' victory target came down to single figures. Flintoff had run out of heroic deeds for the match and it was left to Harmison to bowl with four runs required. The first ball of the over was an attempted yorker which ended up being a full toss that Lee sent fizzing through the covers. There were cheers from the Australians in the crowd, believing it was destined for the ropes, but it was only a single as it soon became clear England had a fielder positioned close to the boundary.

Three to win; Kasprowicz on strike. Harmison bowls. A short-pitched ball rears up at the No. 11 who tries to fend it off but can only glove it to Geraint Jones behind the stumps, who dives low to his left to claim the catch and win the match for England. Edgbaston erupted. Grown men wept. Children were hoisted high into the sky like cricket balls after a catch has been taken – except one can only hope parents waited to claim them from gravity's pull. Vaughan jumped into Flintoff's arms and pulled his ears. It seemed like the whole world was jumping up and down. In that moment, England had not only won the match, they'd gone a long way to winning back the Ashes as they rediscovered their belief.

The third Test at Old Trafford was every bit as nail-biting. England again established a large first-innings lead, eventually setting the tourists 423 to win. This time, Ponting stood in England's way with a spellbinding knock of 156. When he was the ninth man out, Australia had 354 on the board but four overs still to survive on the final day. This time, McGrath and Lee were the final pair and they managed to hold on to scrape a draw. After the agony of coming so close to victory at Edgbaston, this felt like a victory for the tourists, with Lee celebrating wildly – he had famously been consoled by Flintoff in Birmingham, but this time he had won, well drawn. 'I was delighted to see Australian players on the balcony hugging each other because they'd drawn, not won a game,' said Vaughan. The tide was really turning.

England continued to dominate in the next match at Trent Bridge, with the Aussies – again missing McGrath – being forced to follow on. These really were heady days for England cricket fans. They made a better fist of their second innings, leaving England to make 129 to win the match and take a series lead. At 103 for four, England were coasting but, 23 balls later, they were 116 for seven. However, Giles and Matthew Hoggard held their nerves to see England home as a nation rejoiced. With England 2-1 up with one Test to play, everything was still on the line at The Oval.

England had made 373 thanks to 129 from Andrew Strauss, but Australia were on course to sail past that total at 264 for one, with Langer and Matthew Hayden both making tons. Not for the first time, Flintoff then changed the course of the game by removing Ponting, Damien Martyn, Hayden and Simon Katich, and the Aussies were all out six runs short of England's total.

As bad light threatened Australia's chances of making early breakthroughs in England's second innings, the crowd played their part with England's Barmy Army raising umbrellas to try to convince the umpires it was raining, while their Aussie counterparts all removed their shirts and put on sunglasses to suggest otherwise. It had been that kind of series.

On a dramatic final day, England were twice in trouble at 126 for five and 199 for seven, with plenty of time for the tourists to reel off the runs that would have been required and cling on to the urn. But Kevin Pietersen was in no mood for the party to be spoilt and his memorable 158, assisted by Giles who batted for close to three hours for his 59, saved the match and sent a nation delirious with cricket joy for the first time in almost 19 long years.

England had not only won the Ashes, but also a new generation of cricket fans. The open-top bus parade that followed the next day was excessive and deservedly so – it was a fitting way to end the most exciting Ashes Test series of all.

But spare a thought for the wife of the England captain, Mrs Nichola Vaughan. As her husband reflected at the end of the series: 'I've probably been a nightmare to live with throughout the whole summer – my wife's not really got much conversation out of me at all.'

● 4. BRADMAN'S ASHES – 1930

If the 1981 series is referred to as Botham's Ashes, there is no good reason why the 1930 Ashes is not known as Bradman's. So from this point on, it is.

This was Bradman's first Ashes tour, and it's fair to say he announced himself in a rather spectacular fashion. In fact, it's fair to say that he was a bit of a show-off, such were his extraordinary achievements with the bat.

Although England won the opening Test, the Don still managed to score 131 in his side's losing cause and he followed that up with 254 at Lord's as Australia won by seven wickets to square the series. *Wisden* noted of Bradman's display: 'In obtaining his 254, the famous Australian gave nothing approaching a chance. He nearly played on at 111 and, at 191, in trying to turn the ball to leg he edged it deep into the slips but, apart from those trifling errors, no real fault could be found with his display.'

He followed up that trick by striking an unbeaten 309 on the opening day of the third Test at Headingley, finishing on 334 in a drawn match of which *Wisden* wrote: 'Truly could it be called Bradman's match.' (We went one better by giving him the series).

A rain-affected drawn Test at Old Trafford was the only match of the series in which Bradman did not score a century. This set up a decider at The Oval in which the batting maestro's 232 helped Australia score 695 to surpass England's 405, before bowling out the hosts for 251 to win by an innings and 39 runs and regain the Ashes.

By the time the Aussies had secured the urn, Bradman had struck 974 runs in the series at an average of 139.14. Not bad for a first-timer.

● 5. THE BOUNCER WAR – 1974-75

When Tony Greig aimed a short-pitched delivery at Dennis Lillee's head during the first innings of the first Test, he had no idea what he was starting. Lillee was caught behind and felled all at the same time, but a rather lethal fuse had been lit and some spectacular fireworks were about to start.

Lillee recalled: 'He's given me the message that there's a nice cold shower waiting for me in the pavilion, so as I went past him I said: "Just remember one thing. Remember who started this."'

The bowler was raging and he repeated his menacing words in the dressing room to skipper Ian Chappell: 'Remember who started this.'

When England batted, Lillee and Jeff Thomson rained down a series of monumentally rapid red leather missiles at them, and saved their best for Greig. 'It was ridiculous,' says Thomson. 'We were trying to kill him [Greig] and that was the first time I'd ever seen Ian Chappell filthy. He had a go at Dennis and I.'

Greig made a memorably defiant century in that innings, but that was to be the last time he, or England, held any sort of upper hand in the series as the two pacemen wreaked havoc on the tourists, who cowered before their might in a Bodyline role reversal.

'Those days they only had a cap on, compared to these days coming out like Sir Lancelot, so I suppose that makes a bit of a difference to it,' says Thomson, barely trying to conceal the smirk on his face.

The onslaught continued throughout the series as Australia powered to a 4-1 triumph – the same score by which England had won the Bodyline series. Each contest was played with the same level of intensity; there was no let-up from Lillee and Thomson. When Lillee was struck again by Greig, who was then applauded by teammate Keith Fletcher, the Aussie warned him: 'It'll be your turn soon.'

And he wasn't joking either, as England's David Lloyd recalls: 'When it was Fletcher's turn the following day, Lillee walked him in! He went right across to the gate and walked in with Fletch. And he almost took guard with him in front of the stumps!'

By the end of the series Lillee and Thomson starred in a famous *Sydney Telegraph* cartoon with a rhyme that was quickly adopted by all Aussie cricket fans:

Ashes to Ashes, dust to dust,

If Thommo don't get you, then Lillee must.

● 6. THE CORONATION ASHES – 1953

That whole feel-good summer of 2012, in which the Queen's Diamond Jubilee celebrations were followed by the Olympics and a British sporting success story was not unique – despite everything you may have read to the contrary.

June 1953 saw the young Queen Elizabeth's Coronation begin the month, followed by the news of Edmund Hillary and Sherpa Tenzing's successful conquest of Mount Everest. A buoyant nation then turned its celebratory attention to the Ashes, as England attempted to wrestle back the urn that they had last held by winning the Bodyline series two decades earlier.

The opening Test at Trent Bridge was drawn as a day lost to rain meant England ran out of time in their pursuit of 229 to win; they were left frustrated on 120 for one.

The nation then held its collective breath, as England looked set for defeat at Lord's at 73 for four before lunch on the final day, chasing an unlikely 343 for victory. But Trevor Bailey joined Willie Watson in a memorable partnership, with the pair batting for more than four hours to save the game as millions tuned in on wirelesses across the land. Bailey had extra help, though – or should that be an extra helping? – as he ate both his and Watson's lunch.

Two more draws, at Old Trafford and Headingley, followed and the tension couldn't have been greater as the series headed to a decider at The Oval.

And the nation wasn't to be disappointed as England's new spin pair of Tony Lock and Jim Laker took nine second-innings wickets to set up victory after both sides had made moderate first-innings totals. England were left needing 132 for victory and Denis Compton hit the winning runs to spark jubilant scenes as he and Middlesex colleague Bill Edrich were swamped by fans, who then made their way to the pavilion and chanted 'We want Len' in reference to England captain Hutton. Which is far more genteel than some of the songs the Barmy Army have come up with in recent times.

7. BACK-TO-BACK NAIL-BITERS – 1902

The 1902 series may have lacked a Match of the Century (it might have been a bit early in the century to call it that anyway), but it did feature two of the closest Ashes matches in history. After two rain-affected draws at Edgbaston and Lord's, the tourists took first blood with a convincing 143-run victory in a low-scoring match at Sheffield's Bramall Lane, the only time the venue was used for a Test.

Then came a vital game at Old Trafford, with the urn very much on the line. This was the match that became known as 'Tate's Test' in some circles because of the crucial role played by 'one-hit wonder' Fred Tate (*see* Top 10 Australia Ashes Heroes). His crucial dropped catch meant Australia were able to set England 124 to win when it might have been much less. Incredibly, it was Tate who was last man in with England needing four runs to win, but he succumbed to the pressure and the tourists claimed the win and the Ashes.

Even though there was nothing other than pride to play for in the final Test, it wasn't played out in that way, with a finish even more thrilling than in Manchester. Australia were in the ascendancy with a 141-run first-innings lead, but they collapsed to 121 all out, leaving England an unlikely 263 to win. It was even less likely when the home side were 48 for five, but Gilbert 'The Croucher' Jessop blazed his way to 104 in just 75 minutes and gave them hope. But once he was out, wickets started to fall again and, at 214 for eight, England looked buried. But George Hirst and Dick Lilley added 34 before the latter was out with 15 still required. 'We'll get 'em in singles,' said Hirst to No. 11 Wilf Rhodes as he arrived at the wicket and, save an edged four and two runs from an overthrow, that's exactly what they did as England crawled to the narrowest of victories by one wicket.

The Ashes were still lost, but as *Wisden* wisely noted: 'In its moral results the victory was a very important one indeed, as no one interested in English cricket could have felt other than depressed and low spirited if all the Test matches played out to a finish had ended in favour of [Australia captain Joe] Darling's team.'

8. MATCH OF THE CENTURY – 1894-95

It may have lacked the physical brutality of 1932-33 or 1974-75, but England's 1894-95 tour of Australia was exciting enough for Queen Victoria herself to demand she be updated on the state of play.

The tour had started with an astonishing Test in Sydney in which England somehow recovered from a 261-run first-innings deficit. Following on, they scored 437 to set Australia 177 to win and, thanks to six for 67 from a hungover Bobby Peel (*see* Close of Play), squeezed home by ten runs. No Test team would win after following on again until, er, England did it at Headingley in 1981.

Then, in the second Test, England capitulated to 75 all out after Australia's captain George Giffen became the first skipper to insert the opposition in Test cricket. The Aussies made only 123 at the end of an unforgettable first day's play and, once again, England's second innings set up victory as they amassed 475, which proved too much for the hosts.

England were cruising to the urn, only for Australia to call up youngster Albert Trott, whose eight for 43 in England's second innings (to add to his 110 undefeated runs in the match) helped the hosts win the next Test by a massive 382 runs. Worse was to come in the fourth Test for the tourists, as England were bowled out for just 65 and 72 in reply to Australia's 284, meaning the series was all-square going into the decider at Melbourne.

This game was hyped as the 'Match of the Century' and *Wisden* reported great numbers of people travelling thousands of miles across the country to witness the occasion. Back in London, Her Majesty was keen to be kept informed of developments throughout and she would no doubt have been delighted to hear England edge a thrilling, seesaw match by six wickets, successfully chasing down 297 to win the series 3-2.

9. THE BIRTH OF THE ASHES – 1882

This wasn't even an Ashes series – it was a one-off Test match at The Oval that gave birth to the Ashes, which makes it more than suitable for inclusion in this chapter.

Fred 'The Demon' Spofforth was the man who made England pay when W.G.Grace unfairly ran out Sammy Jones, who had left his crease to pat down the wicket believing the ball was dead – he wouldn't do that against Grace or England again. The Aussie bowler was incensed and followed up his first-innings seven-wicket haul with another seven as England, chasing just 85, could muster only 77 all out from a position of 51 for two.

It was all too much for poor George Spendlove, not a name synonymous with the Ashes, but one that should be because he was the spectator that day in south London for whom the tension became just too much and he dropped down dead with heart failure. Another fan, who bit through his umbrella handle, didn't realise how lightly he had got off.

As happy as the tourists must have been, none of them realised how that one match would be placed in a historical context forever, as the placing of the famous faux obituary in the *Sporting Times* ensured every contest between the countries would be played for the ashes of English cricket, which had died at The Oval thanks to Australia's unlikely seven-run victory.

Were it not for that prank, the teams might well have been playing for the George Spendlove Trophy or even the Golden Umbrella ...

Australia win in 1882 on the smallest wicket in Ashes history.

● 10. THE FIRST ASHES WHITEWASH – 1920-21

The 1920-21 series didn't make for a thrilling spectacle. There were no close finishes, no deaths in the crowd and no gnawed umbrella handles. What there was, was an Australian machine that knew only how to win and rewrote the record books by dishing out the first Ashes whitewash to England – sadly, Glenn McGrath wasn't around to predict that one, but no doubt his grandfather called it.

Without an Ashes win since 1909 – mainly due to the Great War interrupting – this was a long-awaited success, although nobody would have imagined how emphatic the victory would be.

After tumbling to a 377-run defeat in the opening Test, England were always going to be up against it and another heavy defeat, by an innings and 91 runs, followed at Melbourne.

Captain Johnny Douglas, a man known for his pig-headedness, didn't help England's cause. He frequently overbowled himself and was doing just that in the Melbourne Test from the Scoreboard End, which featured all the bowling figures. Legend has it that teammate Cec Parkin called to him: 'Mr Douglas, if you won't stop bowling, put yourself on at the other end where you can read your analysis!' The Australians had their own nickname for Douglas, who became known as 'Johnny Won't Hit Today' on account of his infamously dour batting, and his excessive number of initials.

And Douglas's mood didn't lighten in the third Test. Although England put on a vastly improved performance at Adelaide, they still came up short, as Warwick Armstrong, who notched his second ton of the series, was one of four Australian centurions in the match.

Another Armstrong hundred and Arthur Mailey's nine for 121, to go alongside his four wickets in the first innings, made it 4-0 before England's misery was completed where it had all begun, at Sydney, with a nine-wicket stroll for Armstrong's team. *Wisden* noted that: 'Their fifth victory in one season set up a record that may never be beaten.' That was reckoning without the 2006-07 side, who were hell-bent on revenge for losing in 2005.

One interesting footnote to this extraordinary series was the way Armstrong set his fields, as he rarely had more than two fielders on the off side. Everyone else was stationed on leg, and this example was used by Douglas Jardine to defend his 'leg theory' tactics in the Bodyline series a decade later. However, with all the runs the Aussies piled up in this series, Armstrong's field was the least of Douglas's worries, as he returned to England as the first captain, but certainly not the last, to be completely humiliated Down Under.

MY FAVOURITE
ASHES MOMENT

talkSPORT PRESENTER
AND FORMER ENGLAND
ALL-ROUNDER
RONNIE IRANI

'My favourite Ashes moment has to be Botham's Ashes in 1981. Not just the Headingley Test, but the whole series was just unbelievable. Ian Botham was brilliant. He came in and did the business. He'd had a torrid time as captain, but he came back and turned the whole series on its head. I've got great memories of seeing him smacking the ball around at Headingley, hooking off his nose at Old Trafford without even looking up and smacking it on to the railway track.

'But Botham was a top, top bowler. First and foremost, he was a big, strong strapping bowler – a match-winner with the bat no doubt – but people forget how great a bowler he was. His record was phenomenal. Beefy charging in, letting the batsman have it. He had the lot. Having said that, I know it was Botham's Ashes, but Bob Willis on that last day at Headingley was absolutely immense, steaming down that hill and knocking the Aussies over. People have always remarked about that look in Bob's eyes and asked what he was on that day. I had a beer with him once and asked him. "All I was on was adrenalin," he told me.

'I can also remember Richard Ellison swinging the ball really well in 1985. He hadn't played much Test cricket, but he came in and swung the ball round corners. He took to Allan Border and gave him real problems. It was a brilliant series which will always stay in my memory, but people soon forgot Ellison even though the guy almost single-handedly turned that Ashes series around for England.'

With his hands full,
Botham needed help to
make sure no drinking
time was wasted.

CHAPTER EIGHT

AUSTRALIA'S ALL-TIME TACHES XI

Debate all you like about who would be in an Aussie all-time Ashes XI, but please do that in your own time. Here, we present the far more important business of the first-ever Australia Taches XI, with players selected purely on the basis of the growth on their upper lip. As the Aussie cricket team song 'Under the Southern Cross' kind of goes, 'Australian moustaches – you f**king beauties!'

● 1. JOE DARLING

A tache that played in 31 Ashes Tests up to 1905, Darling's is surely the finest ever to be worn on the face of an Australia captain.

● 2. MERV HUGHES

More of a face than an actual tache, this one became so synonymous with Hughes that it was only later in life that people realised he also had eyes, nose and mouth.

● 3. HUGH TRUMBLE

Rumours that the off-spinner also used to use this beauty as a pipe cleaner have not been confirmed. We wonder if he and skipper Darling ever had a tache face-off.

● 4. ERNIE JONES

One of the fastest bowlers of all time, he would have been the very quickest had it not been for all that extra weight he carried on his lip.

● 5. MITCHELL JOHNSON

This frankly embarrassing Movember effort has been included only because it's so utterly lamentable. Most newborn baby boys have better taches.

● 6. ROD MARSH

If you look closely you'll notice that this really is a moustache of two halves, each of them as manly and impressive as the other.

● 7. DAVID BOON

The Walrus, arguably the greatest cricketing tache of them all, helped Boon claim his '52 beers on an Ashes flight' record by soaking up at least 49 of them.

● 8. DENNIS LILLEE

Would he really have claimed a then world record 355 Test wickets in 70 matches without this finely coiffeured tache? Not a chance.

● 9. JACK BLACKHAM

It takes an impressive tache to stand out on a beard. The wicketkeeper wore old-fashioned flimsy gloves, but used his monstrous facial hair to snare most victims, and he set standards in the very first Test for the rest to follow.

● 10. IAN CHAPPELL

It takes some front to wear a football goal around your mouth and pretend your teeth are the net, but the Aussie captain got away with it.

● 11. MAX WALKER

The less-heralded member of the terrifying trio of Lillee, Thomson and er, whatsisname, wore a marvellous moustache that, like him, deserves more recognition.

MY FAVOURITE ASHES MOMENT

ENGLAND FIELDER
GARY PRATT

In the fourth Test of 2005 at Trent Bridge, Australia were following on and had reached 155 for two to trail by around 100 runs. Batting alongside Damien Martyn was captain Ricky Ponting, unbeaten on 48 and looking set for a big score, as he attempted to drag his side back into the match in a series that was tied at 1-1. But he hadn't bargained on England's super-sub Gary Pratt, who was fielding at cover point:

'We were at the stage of the game where we had to get a bit of pressure on and take a wicket. I was at cover point, which is a pretty important position in any game. You're always looking for something to just drop and get that run-out chance. Fortunately for me, Damien Martyn hit it a bit too hard and it came quite firm at me. I just picked it up, took aim and thankfully it hit. It's what you dream about really. That was probably one of the first times I'd hit all season, so it was pretty unfortunate for Ponting.

'It went to the third umpire and Alim Dar was nodding his head, so all the lads kind of knew it was out, but you don't want to get carried away until it's up on the big screen.'

'Ponting was livid. Not just because he was out, but also because he was furious at the way England had used substitutes throughout the series. And as he walked up the pavilion steps, he threw a verbal volley aimed towards England coach Duncan Fletcher on the hosts' dressing-room balcony.

'I knew something was going on because [Matthew] Hoggard had a few words with Ponting on the way off, so I knew something was kicking off, and then he was looking up to the balcony. But apparently Duncan Fletcher didn't even see the incident as he was in the toilet! So Ponting was ranting and raving and I don't think Fletcher knew what was happening.

'At the end of the day, you've got to bend the rules to your advantage. I'm sure if Australia were in Australia, they'd be doing the same thing.

What made it worse on this occasion was that Simon Jones was actually in hospital, he was absolutely knackered – it wasn't as if he came off and had a shower and shave. It was a genuine injury, so it [Ponting's reaction] looked a bit bad from that point of view.

'I sat down and had a chat with Ricky after the final Test at The Oval and we had a bit of a laugh. He gave me a couple of pairs of his boots and signed a couple of photographs – he was an out-and-out great bloke, really. I have a lot of respect for him as a captain and a player; he'll go down as one of the greats. To have been a part of an Ashes series where I affected it a little bit, that's quite good on my part.'

So, what happened next for England's super-sub?

'I was at breakfast the morning after [England secured the Ashes] and Vaughany just came up and said: "Look, you're coming with us on the bus." I replied: "Oh, aye brilliant!" That was pretty much it. It was amazing to see the scenes and the amount of people that turned out. The whole series really got everybody involved in cricket.

'I went on to play a bit of football for Crook Town in the Northern League, which was a pretty tough, high standard – it doesn't help when you've got Sky cameras coming to the football games, it doesn't bode well for sliding tackles. I'm also captain of Minor Counties side Cumberland and I work by selling cricket equipment as well. It's hard to get away from it [the run out], when people who know about cricket are coming in to the shop and I'm trying to sell them a cricket bat – it's hard for them not to bring it up in conversation. I tend to want to forget about it and get on with it and just have it in the back of my mind.'

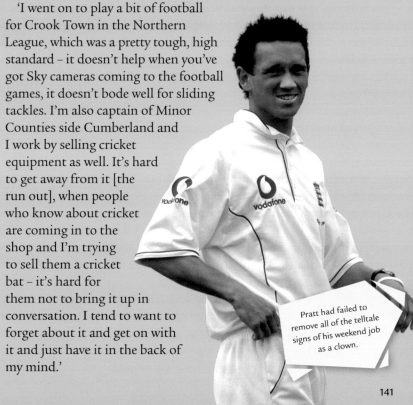

Pratt had failed to remove all of the telltale signs of his weekend job as a clown.

CHAPTER NINE

ENGLAND'S ALL-TIME TACHES XI

The Ashes rivalry was not played out just on cricket pitches. It was also firmly contested in front of bathroom mirrors, at high-end gentlemen's grooming salons and, when all else failed, with a Charlie Chaplin stick-on accessory. The England teams took the Aussies' rampant upper-lip growths seriously as you can see from this MCC taches XI.

● 1. ANDREW STODDART

Underneath the monster hairy slug, you'll find an England captain who once scored 485 batting for Hampstead after an all-night poker session. You can't do that with a smooth upper lip.

● 2. JACK RUSSELL

The wicketkeeper-turned painter was always something of an artist, if you consider his immaculately kept, thick, trademark moustache.

● 3. BOBBY PEEL

One of England's greatest ever all-rounders, not just because of his batting and bowling, but because of the wonderful turn he managed to elicit from the fine ends of his tache.

● 4. GRAHAM GOOCH

It varied over the years in size, weight and stature, but Gooch's upper lip would never be seen naked in public during his playing career.

5. W.G.GRACE

Turn back the page and have a look at Australia's Jack Blackham. Does he look familiar now? Imitation is the sincerest form of flattery and all that...

6. IAN BOTHAM

The man. The legend. The tache. Like Samson himself, removing Beefy's beautiful mullet and tache combo would mean no Headingley '81 and certainly no Shredded Wheat ads.

7. KEVIN PIETERSEN

England's token Movember inclusion, but KP pulls his off far better than Mitchell Johnson to channel his inner Cary Grant.

8. ALLAN LAMB

Any England cricket XI has to have its fair share of non-Englishmen, so Lamby is a welcome addition with his trim and tidy effort.

● 9. REGINALD 'TIP' FOSTER

The only man to captain England at both football and cricket used to remove the novelty tache before football for fear of receiving a terrible kicking.

● 10. MIKE HENDRICK

The man who almost played instead of Bob Willis at Headingley '81 often used to end up locked in the lions' den at zoos after panicking members of the public.

● 11. GEOFF MILLER

Not only did England's chief selector scoop the catch that won the nail-biting 1982 Melbourne Test, he was also named Derbyshire's Moustached Sports Personality of the Year in 1983.

MY FAVOURITE ASHES MOMENT

talkSPORT CRICKET CORRESPONDENT JACK BANNISTER

'There's one Test that stands out on its own by many a mile. On Bob Willis's tour of Australia in 1982-83, the Boxing Day Test at Melbourne went down to the wire. Half an hour from the end of the fourth day, England took the ninth Australian second-innings wicket, with the hosts still needing 74 to win. England had Jeff Thomson, the No. 11, to bowl at, so Willis deliberately gave the out-of-form Allan Border singles so they could bowl at Thomson.

'By the end of that day, Australia had scored 37 of those runs, and the following morning Willis still gave Border the singles to get him off strike. In what turned out to be the penultimate over, Willis had miscounted and thought he'd finished after five balls, so had to bowl another one to keep Border there so Thomson would have the strike for the next over – which he did.

'So that left Botham to bowl to Thomson – Australia just wanted one snick for four and the game was over, England would have lost the Test match. Thomson got a nick; Chris Tavaré dropped it at slip and put his head in his hands. Meanwhile, somehow, Geoff Miller ran round behind him and caught the rebound – England had won by three runs. As they galloped off the field, the players turned round and saw Tavaré, who was aware they'd won the game, but was still horrified and ashen-faced that he'd dropped what could have been the vital catch.

'Live television in Australia actually missed the moment because they hadn't come back after the commercial break – it was quite a cock-up!'

During leaner periods of Ashes success, England always celebrated dot balls.

CHAPTER TEN

27 USELESS ASHES TRIVIA NUGGETS

If your friends don't think you're weird and boring enough already because of your cricket obsession, this chapter will send you right over the edge in their eyes. For this is the ultimate collection of utterly useless, weird, bizarre and frankly stupid facts about the Ashes that any fan could possibly wish to own. If it's not in here, then it's definitely not weird and useless enough. Prepare to nerd yourself right up.

When England won back the Ashes for the first time in 1882-83, the series wasn't actually over. A fourth match was played which experimented with playing each innings on a different batting strip. Australia won it, meaning the final series score was actually 2-2.

The first player to have represented both England and Australia in Ashes Tests was Billy Midwinter (once kidnapped by W.G.Grace – see Ashes Fever). He played for the Aussies in the first two official Tests in 1876-77 and then returned to his English birthplace and turned out against Australia on the England tour of 1881-82. Having tasted action for both teams, he opted to represent Australia for the rest of his career. The other four were John Ferris, Billy Murdoch, Albert Trott and Samuel Woods.

Australia captain Billy Murdoch has the distinction of being the only man to ever catch out his own batsman in an Ashes Test. When W.G.Grace injured a finger in the field in the 1884 Lord's Test, Murdoch helped out his friend by fielding for him and subsequently snared the catch that removed his side's top scorer, 'Tup' Scott.

The entire Australia team refused to play in the second Test at Melbourne in 1884-85 due to a dispute over their share of gate money. Rather than yield to their demands, the selectors simply replaced the entire team for the match, which England won by ten wickets.

Australia all-rounder Tom Garrett became the only man to officiate in an Ashes Test match in which he was also playing. During the 1884-85 series, Garrett had to step in to replace J.H.Hodges, who refused to continue after several England complaints about him.

The 1888 Ashes Old Trafford Test remains the shortest ever played in England. After the hosts posted 172, the tourists were dismissed for 81 and 70 by 1.52pm on day two – a total playing time of six hours 34 minutes. (In those days, you followed on with any first-innings deficit of 80 or more.)

In 1909, the England selectors used 25 different players during the 2-1 home Ashes series defeat. This included making five changes for the second Test, despite England winning the first by ten wickets!

The record for the number of players used by one team during an Ashes series is held by England with 29 in the six-Test summer of 1989. David Gower and wicketkeeper Jack Russell were the only players to feature in every game for England, whose selectors refused to pick players that had opted to join the South Africa rebel tour that winter. The result was 4-0 to Australia.

The 1912 Ashes was the only occasion in which the urn was contested as part of a three-way tournament with South Africa. Each country played the other three times, with the results of the England v Australia matches counting towards the Ashes, which England won.

The world's greatest batsman™ Don Bradman endured a nightmare Ashes debut as he failed twice with the bat in Australia's huge 675-run defeat at Brisbane in 1928-29. Not only that, he was subsequently dropped for the only time in his career.

When England notched up their highest-ever score of 903 for seven declared at The Oval in 1938, captain Wally Hammond had intended to bat on to 1,000 but took pity on the tourists who were physically drained and had suffered two injuries in the field to Jack Fingleton and Bradman.

That 1938 Oval match saw an Ashes (and all Tests) record victory margin of an innings and 579 runs by England; it also saw left-arm spinner Leslie Fleetwood-Smith concede a record 298 runs.

England off-spinner John Emburey was the hero of the 1979 Adelaide Test when he saved the life of Australia opener Rick Darling. The gum-chewing batsman was struck on the chest by a lethal Bob Willis delivery and collapsed with the gum stuck in his throat. Emburey's swift thump on the back dislodged the gum, and Darling started breathing again.

 Australia's Bob Massie holds the record for the best-ever bowling figures by a Test debutant as he took an astounding eight wickets in each innings of the 1972 Lord's Test to finish with 16 for 137, the best figures by an Australian in the Ashes.

As he released the ball, the remaining three buttons on Massie's shirt fell off.

In 1953, England's Len Hutton became the only captain to lose the toss in all five Tests of a series and still emerge victorious.

The Centenary Test of 1977, which was played to mark the anniversary of the first official Test between England and Australia in 1877, was won by the Aussies by 45 runs. The result of the original 1877 game? – a 45-run win for Australia.

Reginald 'Tip' Foster is one of those names worth remembering for irritating pub-quiz questions. Not only is he the record holder for making the highest score on debut, with 287 in the 1903-04 Sydney Test, he's also the only man to have captained England at both cricket and football.

After the miracle of Headingley in 1981, the England players were in celebratory mood in their dressing room but had no champagne. The Australians had been on course for victory at the beginning of the day and had the bubbly ready, so England's management negotiated a price for a few bottles and the England players toasted their success with the Aussies' champagne.

England suffered an extraordinary injury jinx during the 1994-95 Ashes tour, with only four of the original 16-man squad reporting fit for every game. Six players had to leave the tour due to injury, while another half-dozen missed games with a variety of knocks or illnesses. Physio Dave Roberts put the cherry on the icing on the cake when he suffered a broken finger in fielding practice.

The Bodyline series of 1932-33 and England's predominant use of leg-side fields led to the rule change that prevents a fielding team from having any more than two fielders positioned behind square leg.

The high-trousered XI always drew a full house to their fixtures.

In the 1953 Trent Bridge Ashes Test, England's Alec Bedser not only picked up astonishing match figures of 14 for 99, he also secured the record for the best bowling figures by a member of the losing team.

 Australians William Henry Cooper (born 1849) and Paul Sheahan (born 1946) are the only great-grandfather and great-grandson pair to play Ashes or Test cricket.

 It's fair to say England captain Stanley Jackson had a half-decent Ashes series in 1905. Not only did England win 2-0, but Jackson was top of both the batting and bowling averages and won the toss in all five matches.

 Aussie batsman Syd Gregory holds the unwanted record for most ducks in the Ashes with 11 big fat zeroes.

 England wicketkeeper John Murray once took an Ashes record 80 balls to get off the mark while batting with an injured shoulder in the 1962-63 Sydney Test. Australia's record holder is Carl Rackemann, who took 76 balls to score a run at Sydney in 1991.

 Three players have been dismissed for 'diamond ducks' (run out without facing a ball) in Ashes Tests. The hapless trio are: England's William Attewell at Sydney in 1884-85; Rodney Hogg at Edgbaston in 1981; and Simon Katich at Adelaide in 2010-11.

 England managed to score just 19 runs in one dour session of the Brisbane Test in 1958-59. Trevor Bailey led the rearguard action by scoring just eight throughout the morning, and finished with a mind-blowingly stoic 68 made from 425 balls in 458 minutes. And England still lost.

MY FAVOURITE
ASHES MOMENT

AUSTRALIA FAST BOWLER
MERV HUGHES

'The time that really stands out was 1989, when we had Geoff Lawson and Terry Alderman in the side. They were the senior, experienced bowlers at the time.

'I remember in the Lord's Test match: England batted first and made 286, we made 528. In England's second innings, Robin Smith and David Gower were batting well and it was coming to that time when England were about 100 or 120 runs behind and it could have got quite nasty.

'I came back on, and I was bowling at David Gower – not *to* David Gower, I was bowling *at* him. He was a little bit poppy on the back foot, so I said to Allan Border at mid-on that with the length I was bowling I don't need a mid-on and if I had a leg gully, I might be able to jam him up and get an edge.

'I reckon about three balls later, I jammed him up, he got an edge and was caught by Border at leg gully, or shortish backward square leg. There are two things about that which still amaze me to this day: one, that I actually thought about how to get a wicket and two, that Allan Border actually listened to me!

'But that's what kind of captain he was. He'd ask you what you were thinking as a bowler. He was the greatest asset I had. He was a fantastic leader, he led from the front and was one of the most determined and courageous players I ever played with. A lot of people don't remember that before the '89 Ashes tour, he'd played in England for three years and he had a dossier on each player. When anyone came into the side, Border had specific plans for each batsman.

'When you've got a bloke prepared to go that far, and have a skipper like that, it just made life a lot easier. He'd back you to the hilt, both on and off the ground. If you went through a tough patch and the media were on your back, then Border would defend you. I can honestly say he's the biggest asset I ever had through my career.'

Hughes chuckled to himself as he prepared to bowl the rotten tomato.

THE 10 BEST ASHES HEADLINES

In recent times, Australian and English newspaper headline writers have been able to join in the fight for the Ashes with their amusing verdicts on the action. They may not win the urn themselves, but they certainly warrant inclusion here.

● 1.

IT'S NOT OVER TILL THE FAT LADDIE SPINS

The *Sun* urging England to beware of Shane Warne going into the final Test of 2005.

● 2.

NASSER INSANE

The *Herald Sun*'s take on the England captain's decision to bowl first in the 2002-03 Brisbane Test.

● 3.

IS THAT ALL YOU'VE GOT, SHEILAS?

The *Sun*, after Australia lost to Bangladesh before the 2005 Ashes.

4.

WHAT'S WORSE THAN A WHINGEING ENGLISHMAN ... GLOATING POMMIES

The *Sydney Daily Telegraph*'s response to the *Sun*'s headline.

5.

IS THERE *ANYONE* IN ENGLAND WHO CAN PLAY CRICKET?

The *Sydney Daily Telegraph* after England were bowled out for 79 and thrashed in the first Test of the 2002-03 series.

6.

TEN POUNDED POMS
(PLUS A SOUTH AFRICAN CAPTAIN THEY'LL WANT TO SEND BACK)

Sydney's *Sun-Herald* gets carried away after England are dismissed for 260 on the first day of the 2010-11 series.

7.

WE KICKED THEIR ASHES

The *Sun* after England's 2009 series win.

FISH ROTS FROM THE HEAD

The *Sydney Daily Telegraph* lambasts the Australian top order during the 2010-11 Melbourne Test.

IN AFFECTIONATE REMEMBRANCE OF AUSTRALIAN CRICKET, WHICH DIED AT THE MCG ON 26TH DECEMBER 2010
DEEPLY LAMENTED BY A LARGE CIRCLE OF SORROWING FRIENDS AND ACQUAINTANCES. RIP.

The *Sydney Morning Herald* pays homage to Reginald Brooks' 1882 mock obituary after England retained the Ashes in 2010-11.

SKIPPY, DAME EDNA, KYLIE, ROLF HARRIS ... YOUR BOYS TOOK ONE HELL OF A BEATING!
(OK, MAYBE NOT, BUT IT FEELS LIKE IT)

The *Sun*, after England saved the first Test of 2009 by the skin of their teeth.

● DEDICATION

For Victoria, Jake and Rafi

● ACKNOWLEDGEMENTS AND PICTURE CREDITS

Acknowledgements

Without going into Oscar acceptance speech mode, certain people must be thanked on this page or else, frankly, it would be rude.

So, a huge thanks to the following for their time and contributions: Graham Thorpe, Gary Pratt, Brett Lee, Peter Such, Ronnie Irani, Darren Gough, Jack Bannister, Dean Headley, Jason Gillespie and the one and only Merv Hughes.

Also, a massive thanks to the following people, all of whom helped in equally important ways: Dave Lipscomb, Adrian Phillips, Judie Andersen, Laura Wootton, Danny Reuben, Peter Thompson, Jesse Hogan, James Masters, Rob Badman, Malcolm Knox and You Know Who at the News and Star...

And the following deserve huge applause because without them (and me, but enough about me) this book wouldn't exist: Jonathan Conway, Calum Macaulay, Ian Marshall, Scott Taunton, Craig Stevens and Julian Flanders.

Finally, it's impossible to do justice to the extraordinary love and support given to me by Victoria, Jake and Rafi – thank you to my family, this one's for you.

Picture credits

The Publishers would like to thank the following for providing copyright photographs included in this book:

All photographs © **Getty Images**, except the following: pages 16, 33, 44, 47, 60, 63, 65, 73, 92, 103, 115, 125, 139 (no. 11), 141 and 145 (no. 9) © **PA Photos**.

● BIBLIOGRAPHY

In the course of researching this book, the following resources were used:

The Ashes' Strangest Moments, Mark Baldwin (Robson Books, 2005)
Botham: My Autobiography, Ian Botham (Collins Willow, 1994)
Howzat! Sixteen Australian Cricketers Talk To Keith Butler,
    Keith Butler (Collins, 1979)
The Big Ship, Gideon Haigh (Aurum Press, 2003)
The Book of Ashes Anecdotes, Gideon Haigh (Penguin, 2006)
Cricket My World, Walter R.Hammond (Stanley Paul, 1948)
The Wit of Cricket, Barry Johnston (Hodder & Stoughton, 2009)
The Best of Enemies, Whingeing Poms Versus Arrogant Aussies,
    Patrick Kidd and Peter McGuinness (Know the Score, 2009)
Spinning Around The World, Jim Laker (Sportsmans Book Club, 1959)
Henry: The Geoff Lawson Story, Geoff Lawson (Ironbark Press, 1993)
It's Not Cricket, Simon Rae (Faber and Faber, 2001)
What Now? The Autobiography, Phil Tufnell (Collins Willow, 1999)
*Flying Stumps and Metal Bats: Cricket's Greatest Moments by the People
    Who Were There*, Wisden Cricketer (Aurum Press, 2010)

Weekend Australian magazine
West Australian newspaper
alloutcricket.com
cricinfo.com
smh.com.au
theage.com.au
dailytelegraph.com.au
independent.co.uk
guardian.co.uk
telegraph.co.uk
dailymail.co.uk
mirror.co.uk
thesun.co.uk
bbc.co.uk
skysports.com
youtube.com